World War II
The War in Europe

The
MILITARY HISTORY
of the
UNITED STATES

Christopher Chant

World War II
The War in Europe

MARSHALL CAVENDISH
NEW YORK · LONDON · TORONTO · SYDNEY

Library Edition Published 1992

© Marshall Cavendish Limited 1992

Published by
Marshall Cavendish Corporation
2415 Jerusalem Avenue
PO Box 587
North Bellmore
New York 11710

Series created by Graham Beehag Book Design

Series Editor	Maggi McCormick
Consultant Editors	James R. Arnold
	Roberta Wiener
Sub Editor	Julie Cairns
Designer	Graham Beehag
Illustrators	John Batchelor
	Steve Lucas
	Terry Forest
	Colette Brownrigg
Indexer	Mark Dartford

The publishers wish to thank the following organizations
who have supplied photographs:

The National Archives, Washington. United States
Navy, United States Marines, United States Army,
United States Air Force, Department of Defense,
Library of Congress, The Smithsonian Institution.

The publishers gratefully thank the U.S. Army Military
History Institute, Carlisle Barracks, PA. for the use of
archive material for the following witness accounts:

Pages 112-113
From letter excerps, December 22-29, 1944, 501st
Parachute Infantry Regiment.

Page 114-115
From papers of Sgt. Raymond Burgess, 38th Infantry
Regiment, 2nd Infantry Division.

Library of Congress Cataloging-in-Publication Data

Chant, Christopher.
    The Military History of the United States / Christopher Chant –
Library ed.
        p. cm.
    Includes bibliographical references and index.
    Summary: Surveys the wars that have directly influenced the
    United States., from the Revolutionary War through the Cold War.
    ISBN 1-85435-360-8 ISBN 1-85435-361-9 (set)
    1. United States - History, Military - Juvenile literature.
    [1. United States - History, Military.] I. Title.
    t181.C52 1991
    973 - dc20   90 - 19547
                                                        CIP
                                                        AC

Printed in Singapore by Times Offset PTE Ltd
Bound in the United States

Contents

In the 15 years between 1921 and 1936, the United States remained confident through all levels of society, politics, and the military that war could and should be avoided. The only possible exception was Japan, whose ambitions in the Pacific basin were an increasing source of worry to more far-sighted Americans.

The American public generally believed that the United States could achieve the goal of a peaceful future by maintaining a minimum defensive strength, avoiding any form of political entanglement with the countries of Europe, and using the country's position as a recognized neutral to play a key part in promoting international peace and limiting armaments. The first U.S. initiative in this field was the Washington Naval Conference, which began on November 19, 1921, and lasted until February 6, 1922. The final agreement, called the Washington Treaties, froze the capital ship and aircraft carrier strengths of the United States, the United Kingdom, and Japan in the ratio of 5-5-3.

Combined with restrictions on the building of new naval bases, this agreement made it virtually impossible for the United States and Japan to clash in the Pacific as long as the agreement's terms were not breached. It also made any effective American defense of the Philippines impossible, but Japan made a general agreement with the western powers not to upset the status quo in the Pacific and eastern Asia. This accord indicated that Japan would not start on a war of aggression.

Between June and August 1927, a so-called Three-Power Naval Conference was held in Geneva, Switzerland, between the United States, the United Kingdom, and Japan. It tried unsuccessfully to go a step beyond the Washington Treaties by setting up a ratio for cruisers, destroyers, and submarines.

Greater success came from talks held in Paris during 1928. Otherwise known as the Kellogg-Briand Pact, the Treaty of Paris was signed on August 1927 between the United States, the United Kingdom,

Between the World Wars, the U.S. Navy experimented with the use of large rigid airships for long-range reconnaissance. The program spurred considerable interest, but ultimately proved unsuccessful. The airships, some of the finest ever produced, included the American-designed ZR-1 (U.S.S. *Shenandoah*), the British-designed ZR-2 (never delivered as it broke up during a trial flight), the German-designed ZR-3 (U.S.S. *Los Angeles*), and the American-designed sisterships ZRS-4 and ZRS-5 (U.S.S. *Akron* and U.S.S. *Macon*).

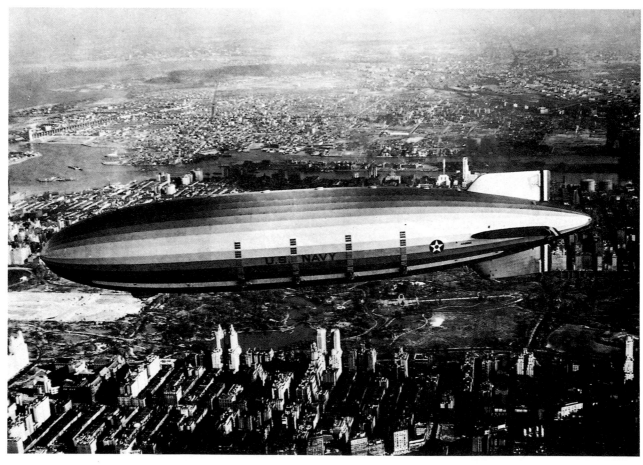

Pouring molten metal in the foundry of the Naval Gun Factory at the Washington Navy Yard. Between the world wars, the United States continued to develop as a major industrial and trading power. The country's self-sufficiency in most strategic aspects of war production was crucial to the Allies during World War II.

France, Italy, Japan, and number of other countries. The treaty committed the signatories to a renunciation of war as an instrument of national policy, but made absolutely no provision for enforcement of the treaty, even by using sanctions. This agreement was the high point of a sincerely believed, but wholly impractical, effort to get these countries, and others, to protect – willingly – the notion of international peace in the period between the world wars. The United States then announced that if other countries would do likewise, she would trim her armed forces to a level low enough only to maintain internal order and protect her own territory against aggression.

Defense of the Nation

This offer in fact included all that the U.S. Army had envisaged in its planning and organization during the 1920s, as the chief of the War Plans Division informed the Chief of Staff in 1931. The army diverged from public and political opinion; it knew that it was too small and

too poorly equipped to undertake even this limited role with a reasonable chance of success.

Meanwhile, international efforts were still being made to reduce, or at least to limit, armament levels. Between January 21 and April 22, 1930, for example, the London Naval Conference led to a treaty signed by the United States, the United Kingdom, France, Italy, and Japan. This agreement regularized submarine warfare, limited submarine tonnage, and fixed the caliber of the guns such boats might carry. Other clauses extended the restrictions already placed on aircraft carriers by the Washington Naval Treaty, established that the United States and the United Kingdom were to scrap certain ships by 1933, and fixed overall tonnages for various classes of warship. The result was to give the United States and Britain equal numbers of cruisers, and to strengthen Japan's position overall.

Already, however, the futility of such efforts was becoming clearer, initially on the far side of the Pacific basin. In 1931, Japan began its seizure of Manchuria

Carefully orchestrated rallies such as this were significant features of German life after the Nazis' rise to power in 1933. They were a powerful propaganda tool gleefully used by the Nazi Party. These rallies helped to recreate a sense of German power and national destiny; as such, they were instrumental in making World War II almost inevitable.

from China, ignoring the diplomatic pressure exerted by the League of Nations and the United States. By 1932, Manchuria had been taken, and Japan was moving against other parts of China as well. (This aggression led eventually to the Sino-Japanese War, which began in 1937.) In May 1933, Japan announced her withdrawal from the League of Nations. She followed this news in December 1934 with the announcement that, in two years' time, she would no longer be bound by the terms of the Washington and London Treaties, due to expire in 1936.

The Re-emergence of Germany

In October 1933, the new Nazi leadership of Germany announced the country's withdrawal from both the League of Nations and the World Disarmament Conference, which had opened in Geneva during 1932. German rearmament had

already started in secret, and in March 1935 Adolf Hitler renounced the disarmament clauses of the Treaty of Versailles imposed on Germany in 1919. At the same time, he announced a huge rearmament program. The nature of German intentions was further revealed by her reoccupation of the Rhineland in March 1936 and her invasion and annexation of Austria in March 1938. In September 1938, she occupied the Sudetenland portion of Czechoslovakia and seized the rump of Czechoslovakia in March 1939, when Bohemia and Moravia were annexed, leaving Slovakia as a nominally independent satellite state. Later in March, she annexed Memel, part of Lithuania.

In Italy, the Fascist party, under Benito Mussolini, forced itself into power at the end of 1922 and signaled its imperialist ambitions with the conquest of Abyssinia (now Ethiopia) between October 1935 and May 1936, when the country was annexed by Italy. Soon an incredibly bitter

The man largely responsible for guiding the United States out of the depression of the early 1930s and then leading the country through World War II was the 31st president, Franklin Delano Roosevelt. Roosevelt did not see the end of the war; he died on April 12, 1945, in Warm Springs, Georgia.

civil war broke out in Spain between forces loyal to the elected republican government and right-wing nationalist forces, led by General Francisco Franco. The war lasted until March 1939, with Franco's Falangist party eventually victorious. The Falangists were politically akin to the Nazis and the Fascists and received enormous help from Germany and Italy. These two countries supported Franco for obvious political reasons, but also found the Spanish Civil War an ideal opportunity to test their latest weapons and their new tactical doctrines under operational conditions.

In October 1936, Germany and Italy created the Berlin-Rome Axis, in which Germany recognized Italy's conquest of Abyssinia and Italy later recognized Germany's annexation of Austria. In November 1936, Germany and Japan signed the Anti-Comintern Pact against the U.S.S.R. The triangle of states that later constituted the Axis powers in the forthcoming World War II was completed in November 1937, when Italy joined the Anti-Comintern Pact and shortly afterward announced her withdrawal from the League of Nations.

A Change in American Policy

It had already become clear that the

Franklin D. Roosevelt
For further references see pages
10, 13, 14, 17, *18*, *20*, 21, 23, *24*, 28, 34, 50, 65, 72, 98, *122*

United States' isolationist position was hampering her efforts in the international arena. In November 1933, the United States recognized the U.S.S.R. and opened diplomatic relations. In 1934 the United States promised eventual independence to the Philippines, and in the same year, the "Good Neighbor" policy toward the Caribbean and Latin America saw the repeal of the Platt Amendment, which had limited Cuba's sovereignty since the country's independence, and the liquidation of American protectorates in the Caribbean.

Between 1934 and 1936, the Nye Committee investigation of the American munitions industry gave an unfortunate impression to many Americans that the United States' entry into World War I had been designed to save the bankers and protect the munitions industry. The hearings therefore had the effect of raising public opposition to larger defense appropriations and of boosting an already strong tendency toward renewed isolationism. An early result was the Neutrality Act, passed by Congress in April 1935, which forbade Americans to supply munitions or loans to foreign belligerents. It also refused American protection to U.S. citizens sailing on the ships of belligerents.

However, knowledge of Japanese aggression in Asia and Italian aggression in Abyssinia, combined with the horrors of the Spanish Civil War, made it clear to the public that the Neutrality Act had gone too far. The War Policy Act, passed by Congress in May 1937, stuck by the mandatory provisions of the Neutrality Act, but also gave President Franklin Delano Roosevelt wide discretion in deciding when to proclaim that a state of war actually existed (the point at which the Neutrality Act's provisions came into effect).

From 1935, U.S. forces began to receive larger appropriations as the deterioration of the world situation became apparent. These appropriations were not large enough for any major expansion, but did allow the existing armed forces to improve their readiness for action. Between 1930 and 1935, General Douglas MacArthur had been Chief of Staff and had devoted much of his time to far sighted planning. Between 1935 and 1938, therefore, the army was able to use its larger appropriations most effectively for a slight increase in strength, a reorganization of its combat forces, and realistic planning of the best way in which the United States could use its manpower and industrial muscle if war became necessary or indeed inevitable.

MacArthur's Far-sighted Vision

The core of MacArthur's recommendation was the creation of a small but very hard-hitting force for emergency use in times of crisis. Essential components of his concept were the mechanization and motorization of all combat units in the regular army and filling existing

Douglas MacArthur
For further references
see pages
22, 29

Douglas MacArthur, seen here in the rank of five-star general, is best remembered as commander of the Southwest Pacific Area in World War II. As a pre-war army chief of staff he played a decisive part in shaping the army that fought in World War II.

ranks so effective training could be undertaken. When the need for new higher command organizations was assessed, the constantly altering nature of modern warfare was also taken into account. These high-command units were intended to supervise the peacetime training of larger air and ground units as well as combined-arms formations, and to assume full command authority in war. So, between 1932 and 1935, the War Department created within the continental United States four army headquarters and the General Headquarters Air Force.

From 1935, these headquarters supervised regular and National Guard formations in major summer maneuvers and other exercises, and in combined operations with elements of the navy. In the same year, Congress authorized an increase in the army's enlisted manpower to 165,000. In the following years, Congress authorized greater spending on accommodation and many types of equipment. The result was a steadily stronger army that was better able to respond both rapidly and flexibly when it

was needed. However, the size and capability of foreign armies had grown much more rapidly over the same period.

The army was now sure that future warfare would be mobile, not the static type that had characterized World War I. At first, there was not enough money available to re-equip the army completely, so the development of the right weapons, ready for mass production when the need arose, was emphasized. Most important were a number of tanks, a new rifle, and an important piece of artillery. The tanks were mainly of the light and medium variety, and were notable for their mechanical reliability, moderately good protection, and high mobility. Although most of these mid-1930s vehicles did not enter mass production, they were effective prototypes for the superb American tanks of World War II. The rifle was the Garand M1 semi-automatic weapon, which was adopted in 1936 to replace the Springfield Model 1903 bolt-action rifle of the same 0.3-inch caliber. The artillery piece was the M2 105-mm howitzer, which entered low-

American infantrymen train in gas warfare during 1943. Gas was not in fact used in World War II, but memories of gas warfare in World War I meant that such training was taken seriously in case the Germans used their huge gas stocks.

The weapon that formed the backbone of the American field artillery in World War II was the 105-mm Howitzer M2A1 on Carriage M2A2. This unexceptional, but thoroughly workmanlike, weapon was one of the types proposed by the Westerveldt Board. This body deliberated in 1919 about the kind of artillery the army would need to replace the miscellany of American and foreign weapons used in World War I. Funding was limited, and the design was not finalized by the Ordnance Department until 1939. Production began in 1940, and 8,536 were produced during the war years. The total rose to 10,202 by the time production ended in 1953. The M2A2 had split trails and pneumatic tires, and proved itself both sturdy and reliable. The M2A1 could fire 13 different kinds of ammunition and was also used in a number of mobile mountings. The complete rig weighed 4,900 pounds, and the traveling dimensions included a length of 19 feet 8 inches, a width of 7 feet 1 inch (increasing to 12 feet in firing position), and a height of 6 feet 6 inches. It took three minutes to bring the gun into action. With a crew of eight, the weapon had a burst firing rate of eight rounds in the first 90 seconds, or a sustained firing rate of 100 rounds an hour.

volume production in 1940 and became the backbone of the American field artillery in World War II.

Mobility of all units and formations was much increased by replacing the horse with the motor vehicle, and tactical mobility was increased by reducing the size of the standard infantry division to little more than half that of its predecessor in World War I. This change, achieved by making the division into a "triangular" formation with three instead of four infantry regiments, was made only after extensive trials.

Industrial Mobilization

It had become clear by 1930 that modern warfare was so complex that an effective war-making capability meant that economic and industrial mobilization had to start at least two years before major formations could be committed to combat. The Industrial Mobilization Plan that year laid the foundations of the United States' national mobilization capability and was refined in 1939. A comparable scheme for manpower was developed in the 1937 Protective Mobilization Plan. The first step of this plan was the induction of the National Guard, creating an Initial Protective Force of about 400,000 men. Together with the navy, this call up was designed to protect the continental United States while the army expanded to the strength required by the circumstances.

An important part of the overall scheme was the development of a full training plan during a time of peace. It included replacement training centers (complete with location, size, and scheduling details), unit training centers, branch schools, individual and unit training programs, and training manuals. The scheme was a very far-sighted effort by the army's planners, and though it was later found to have flaws, its greatest limitation was the fact that the army was thinking in terms of mobilization on the scale of World War I. In fact, more than twice as many men were mobilized during World War II, and, because of the more technological nature of the conflict, several times the industrial effort was needed.

By late 1938, war in Europe was an overwhelming probability rather than a major possibility. On January 12, 1939, President Roosevelt asked Congress to provide $552,000,000 for defense spending. By then, aviation technology had developed enough to impose a new factor on American military thinking: the still unlikely possibility of bombing attacks on the continental United States and the Panama Canal Zone from bases in Europe, or more probably, from forward airfields in Central or South America. Thus, a considerable part of the 1939 appropriation went on increasing not just the defensive, but also the offensive, power of the Army Air Corps.

"Rainbow" Plans

At about the same time, the army and navy began jointly developing the "Rainbow" plans. They took the place of earlier, color-coded plans that were the centerpiece of American defense thinking. The color plans had each been concerned with a defensive war against a single country, but the "Rainbow" plans were wider ranging and covered not just the defense of the United States and her possessions, but hemispheric defense as well. Defense of the western hemisphere remained an army preoccupation until the end of 1940.

On September 1, 1939, German forces invaded Poland, and on September 3, the United Kingdom and France declared war on Germany. World War II had started. On the same day, President Roosevelt addressed the nation in a "fireside chat," saying: "This nation will remain a neutral nation, but I cannot ask that every American remain neutral in thought as well." Two days later, an American state of neutrality was declared, and three days later still, a state of limited national emergency, which permitted an increase in the strengths of the regular army and National Guard to 227,000 and 235,000 men respectively, was proclaimed.

American Industry Shifts Gear

On November 4, Congress followed the president's urging and lifted the arms embargo imposed by the Neutrality Act.

The resulting "cash and carry" export system for munitions and other equipment to the belligerent nations provided a considerable boost to the United Kingdom and France rather than to Germany. A massive flood of orders from Britain and France, together with smaller orders from other countries worried about their position on the periphery of the conflict, helped to shift American war industries toward top gear and paved the way for the massive production levels that played such an important part in the Allied victory in World War II.

After the fall of Poland and the beginning of the "phony war" between Germany and the two western Allies, the pace of American defense preparations slowed. The army, though, still placed great emphasis on improving its ability to respond rapidly to any emergency

The expansion of American industry during World War II was enormous and drew large numbers of women into the workplace. These women, photographed in 1943, were employed in an aircraft factory.

through motorization and the delivery of new equipment. In April 1940, it broke new ground by deploying 70,000 men in the first corps and army level maneuvers ever held in the United States.

In the spring of 1940, the situation in Europe deteriorated dramatically, as Germany struck north to overrun Denmark and Norway from April 9 and then launched a huge offensive to the west from May 10. This strike soon crushed the Netherlands and Belgium and plunged deep into France, which capitulated on June 25. Only the United Kingdom was left to oppose Germany in Europe. In addition, Italy had come into the war on June 10 and now posed a threat to the British position in the Mediterranean and North Africa, including the vital Suez Canal

American Aid for the United Kingdom

This worsening of the European situation

was reflected in the increasing tempo of events in the United States. On January 3 and May 31, 1940, President Roosevelt had called on Congress for military appropriations totaling about $3,400,000,000. On June 3, the president responded to British Prime Minister Winston Churchill's urgent pleas for aid by releasing $43,000,000 worth of surplus arms, munitions, and aircraft. On June 15, a National Defense Research Committee was established under Dr. Vannevar Bush. On June 20, Henry L. Stimson was appointed Secretary of the Army, and Frank Knox was named as Secretary of the Navy. Just two days later, Congress adopted important tax measures designed to improve national defense and also raised the limit of the national debt to $49,000,000,000.

In matters of defense, President Roosevelt relied heavily on General George C. Marshall, the Army Chief of Staff. From the summer of 1940, Marshall was largely responsible, under Stimson's

One of the most decisive factors in World War II was the size and flexibility of the U.S. industrial machine, which produced vast quantities of weapons for the use of the American forces and their allies. The original caption for this 1943 photograph epitomizes the mood of the period: "Stars over Berlin and Tokyo will soon replace these factory lights reflected in the noses of America's fighting planes at Douglas Aircraft's Long Beach, Cal., plant."

political control, for a major expansion intended to guarantee the protection of the United States and the rest of the western hemisphere from external attack, which was thought more likely to come from Europe than from Asia. At the same time, the U.S. Navy also launched a comparable expansion program designed to make it a "two-ocean navy," with the strength to deal simultaneously with a Japanese threat in the Pacific, and a combined German and Italian threat in the Atlantic, should the European Axis powers defeat the United Kingdom.

Both of these programs had considerable popular support, a fact reflected in the size of the congressional appropriations. The army, for example, received for its requirements in the following year the sum of $8,000,000,000, a total larger than all army appropriations in the previous 20 years. An indication of the scale on which the army was now thinking is provided by the munitions program approved on June 30, 1940: it called for the procurement, by October 1941, of all weapons and equipment needed for an army of 1,200,000 men and included provision for a much enlarged and modernized Army Air Corps. By September of the same year, the army was thinking in terms of 1,500,000 men.

A New Draft Law

Clearly the provision of so many men would pose problems, and on August 27, Congress authorized the induction of the National Guard into federal service and the calling up of the Organized Reserves. Then on September 14, 1940, Congress passed the Selective Service and Training Act, which allowed, for the first time in the history of the United States, the drafting of untrained civilians. National Guard units, together with the first draftees and their Reserve officers, were called up as rapidly as camps could be built for them, allowing the army to more than double its strength in the last six months of 1940, and to reach its planned strength of 1,500,000 men by mid-1941.

To control the training of this much expanded army, a new organization was established in July 1940 as the General

Headquarters. At about the same time, the army created the Armored Force as a separate ground combat arm, with training carried out in a separate Armored Force School. Antiaircraft and Tank Destroyer Commands were also created, giving the army seven ground-combat arms, including the Infantry, Field Artillery, Coast Artillery, and Cavalry.

In October 1940, the four army headquarters assumed command of all ground forces in the United States. Under the control of the General Headquarters, they launched a program of intensive all-level training. At this time, the earlier corps area commands were relegated to administration and service. Overseas garrisons were strengthened, and new commands were organized to control the much larger forces being allocated to Alaska and Puerto Rico.

In June 1941, the Army Air Corps became the Army Air Force, and from the following month, General Headquarters was developed into an operational command level for Marshall, in his capacity as

A figure who has perhaps not received all the great public credit due to him, General George Catlett Marshall was the army chief of staff through World War II, who played an absolutely vital part in the conduct of American operations against Germany and Japan. After the war, Marshall was a major figure in the reconstruction of Europe.

Right: Soldiers practice amphibious landing at Camp Bradford, Little Creek, Virginia.

Below: The theory and execution of amphibious operations developed during World War II. A high peak of cooperation between land, naval, and air forces was eventually reached. A key to this success was the creation in the United States of several amphibious warfare training base camps. This photograph taken at Camp Bradford shows soldiers and blue-trousered sailors round an M4 Sherman medium tank during training maneuvers.

A soldier sets an obsolete tank ablaze during chemical warfare training.

Commanding General of the Field Forces.

By the fall of 1941, the U.S. Army had 27 infantry divisions, five armored divisions, two cavalry divisions, and 35 combat air groups. They were the operational core of forces that also contained large support and service elements, as well as other formations and units still undergoing training. This was an enormous advance on the position prevailing just two years earlier, although in terms of operational capability and equipment, this larger American strength was still inferior to that which could be mustered against it by Germany and Japan.

This military expansion was greatly aided by the industrial programs that were already supplying the Allies. In the period between December 20 and 29, 1940, President Roosevelt streamlined the defense effort by creating the Office of Production Management, which was designed to provide aid to Britain and all other countries fighting Germany and Italy at all levels up to, but excluding, war. This effort culminated in the Lend-Lease Act of March 11, 1941, which removed any masking of U.S. support for the Allies. Indeed, its avowed intent was that the United States should become the "arsenal of democracy" waging war against the Axis powers. It was not an altogether altruistic policy, for American political and military leaders were well aware that

I WANT YOU F.D.R. STAY AND FINISH THE JOB!

This 1940 re-election poster supports Roosevelt in a manner that clearly harks back to World War I.

aid to the Allies helped check the spread of the Axis powers, which bought more time for the United States to complete its own defensive measures.

Hemisphere Defense Falters

By this time, the United States was veering away from the concept of hemispheric defense. One of the last vestiges of this policy had been an agreement made with the United Kingdom on September 3, 1940. The U.S. agreed to supply the U.K. with 50 old destroyers in return for air and naval base rights in eight British possessions in the western hemi-sphere, namely Newfoundland, Bermuda, the Bahamas, Jamaica, Antigua, St. Lucia, Trinidad, and British Guiana.

By early 1941, American defense thinking had moved toward a partial, if only passive, involvement in World War II. Many senior army and naval commanders already felt that the United States would be drawn fully into the war in the comparatively near future. Even at this early stage, the commanders agreed on the likelihood of a two-front war, with Japan in the Pacific, and Germany and Italy in the Atlantic or on the mainland of Europe. It was generally agreed that Germany posed a greater military threat to the United States than Japan.

American planners therefore considered the best course to be a war of containment against Japan to allow the major effort to be directed first against Germany. Known as the ''Germany first'' policy, it dovetailed exactly with the political factors that had to be taken into consideration by the government.

The principle was also adopted by American and British military staff representatives, who met in Washington for preliminary talks that ended on March 29, 1941. As a result of these conversations, army and navy planners adapted their most recent grand strategic plan, which was known as ''Rainbow 5,'' to suit the common ground that now existed between the United States and the United Kingdom. Evidence of a shift toward armed neutrality against Germany came with the inauguration of an active naval patrol in the western Atlantic during April and the introduction of air routes across the Atlantic (in the north via Greenland and in the south via Brazil) in June.

Unlimited National Emergency

During this same month, the president was warned by his military advisers that German forces could be preparing a drive into the Iberian peninsula and northwestern Africa. They would then secure Spanish and Portuguese ports which would allow further expansion, to the Azores, Canaries, and Cape Verde island groups. This information, together with German naval activity in the North Atlantic, persuaded the president to issue a proclamation of unlimited national emergency. Within it, the president instructed the army and navy to cooperate in establishing an expeditionary force to

One tactic inherited from World War I was the North Atlantic convoy. The weather was often appalling, and the threat of attack by U-boats was constant but the task was absolutely essential if the United Kingdom was to survive as the Allied springboard for the reconquest of Europe. The U-boats were technically superior to the ones used in World War I. They operated in coordinated ''wolf packs.''

The partnership that guided the United States and United Kingdom through most of World War II was President Franklin D. Roosevelt (seated) and Prime Minister Winston S. Churchill.

Winston Churchill
For further references see pages
14, 28, 33, 34, 50, 65, 72, 98, *122*

be sent to the Azores as a first step in blocking German expansion toward the South Atlantic and possibly South America. Later in the month, however, the president learned that Germany was on the verge of invading the U.S.S.R., which made any foray into the Iberian peninsula and Atlantic most unlikely.

The Germans launched Operation "Barbarossa" on June 22, and within days their armies were deep inside the western U.S.S.R. On April 10, President Roosevelt had announced that Greenland was to come under American military protection, and three days after the Germans moved into the U.S.S.R., American soldiers landed in Greenland, a

first step to the defense of this huge island and the construction of the air bases destined to play a vital part in the air bridge across the North Atlantic. Earlier in the month, the president had decided that American troops would relieve the British forces fulfilling the same task in Iceland; and on July 7, the first American troops arrived on the island, with the full expeditionary force in place by September.

The Atlantic Conference

Between August 9 and 12, Roosevelt and Churchill met for a series of discussions

Even before its entry into World War II, the United States became involved in the conflict when American warships started escorting Allied convoys in the western Atlantic. The first American casualty of this policy was the destroyer U.S.S. *Kearney*, which was torpedoed and damaged on October 16/17, 1941. The photograph shows members of the *Kearney*'s crew inspecting the damage after the ship limped into port.

on board American and British warships anchored in Placentia Bay, Newfoundland. At the end of this so-called Atlantic Conference, the two leaders pledged their nations to preserve world freedom and to improve world conditions after the war. At the same time, Roosevelt announced that American warships would escort all Allied convoys in the North Atlantic as far east as Iceland.

There was still considerable strength in the isolationist movement, however, and the renewal of the Selective Service and Training Act passed the House of Representatives by just a single vote during September.

Pre-war Naval Losses in the Atlantic

The escort system, inaugurated on September 16, had the effect of making the United States a quasi-belligerent. Germany could not let such a move pass without hindrance, and U-boat attacks on two American destroyers followed. The U.S.S. *Kearney* was attacked on October

17, but managed to limp into port. On October 31, the U.S.S. *Reuben James* was attacked and sunk.

These events reduced isolationist inclinations considerably, and in November, Congress voted to repeal the measures that had prevented the arming of American merchant ships and their movement into war areas. The isolationist movement continued as a small, but very vocal, minority, however, and despite general backing for the essentially defensive moves suggested by the president, the American public was not yet ready for a declaration of war that would align the United States with the Allies.

While the American public had been concerned mainly with the threat posed by Germany, events in the Pacific had been moving toward a climax. Throughout the late 1930s and early 1940s, Japan continued to increase her conquests in China; from 1939, she switched her strategy from active conquest to attrition. In the middle of 1940, Japan seized the opportunity offered by Germany's successful campaign in the west to exert pressure on

An early expression of U.S. support for China before and during World War II was the American Volunteer Group. The Chinese air force's Colonel Claire L. Chennault recruited about 100 American pilots to fight for China as mercenaries. The A.V.G. later became known as the "Flying Tigers." After training at a deserted British airfield near Toungoo in Burma, the unit moved into action when Japan launched its offensive in December 1941.

France and the United Kingdom. On June 25, Japan demanded and received French permission to land troops in Indo-China, and the arrival of Japanese warships off Haiphong and other Indo-Chinese ports cut one of China's two surviving lifelines with the outside world, namely the supply route between Haiphong and Kunming. A month later, the Japanese exerted pressure on the British, who agreed on July 18 to close the Burma Road, which was China's only other significant lifeline.

Problems with Japan

On September 4, Secretary of State Cordell Hull warned Japan that any further moves against Indo-China would have a significant detrimental effect on American policy, but 18 days later, Japanese forces began to occupy the northern part of Indo-China. Air bases were soon built, and combined ground and air forces launched yet another Japanese drive into China. Four days after the first landings, the United States banned the export of scrap iron and steel to Japan. As Japan lacked indigenous supplies of these raw materials, this would have a serious effect on the long-term ability of Japanese industry to continue weapons production, and on October 8, Japan branded the embargo an "unfriendly act."

The day after the American embargo had been imposed, the Berlin-Rome-Tokyo Axis was formalized as a ten-year mutual assistance pact.

The Japanese continued to extend their grip on Indo-China, and on July 26, 1941, the United States froze Japanese assets and cut off oil shipments to Japan. At the same time, the War Department recalled General MacArthur to active service and

sent him to command all American and Filipino forces in the Philippines. The islands were also reinforced with additional men and, in a move that was thought to be more important for deterrent purposes, heavy bombers.

On August 17, President Roosevelt warned Japan that continued Japanese efforts toward Asian dominance would force the United States to take measures to safeguard American rights and interests.

All the while, negotiations continued in Washington between the Japanese ambassador and the State Department in an effort to reduce tension between the two countries. Even so, tacit American approval was given for the creation of the American Volunteer Group to provide the Chinese with air support. Led by Captain Claire L. Chennault, the unit, later dubbed the "Flying Tigers," was made up of about 100 ex-service airmen, who flew Curtiss P-40 fighters supplied to China under Lend-Lease arrangements.

Japan Opts for War

Japan decided in principle during September that war with the United States was part of the risk that she would have to run in order to secure dominance in Asia, and with it the major slice of the raw materials and market which this vast and populous region offered. The die was cast in Japan on October 17, when a new military government was formed under General Hideki Tojo. On November 5, the Imperial General Headquarters issued a secret plan for simultaneous offensives against Americans in the Hawaiian Islands and in the Philippines, and the British in Malaya.

On November 15, the Japanese ambas-

Washington D.C.
For further references
see pages
19, 23, 24, 28, 50

A.V.G. pilots rush to their P-40 fighters at the beginning of a scramble against approaching Japanese bombers.

Opposite Top: This photograph shows the explosion that blew off the bow of the destroyer U.S.S. *Shaw*, which was hit by a bomb during the Japanese attack on Pearl Harbor.

Opposite Bottom: President Roosevelt signs the U.S. declaration of war against Japan on December 8, 1941.

A pall of smoke hangs over Pearl Harbor during the attack of December 1941, photographed from a ship at sea south of Oahu Island.

sador in Washington was joined by a special envoy in an effort to secure a resumption of trade negotiations. On November 26, Secretary of State Hull told the two men that the American preconditions included Japan's withdrawal from China and Indo-China and Japanese recognition of Generalissimo Chiang Kai-shek's Kuomintang administration as the rightful government of China. Both conditions were totally unacceptable to Tojo's government, and the military government decided to launch Japan's war as soon as possible. At the same time, talks continued in Washington up to the last minute in order to keep the United States off guard.

Pearl Harbor

On December 7, 1941, the Japanese struck at Pearl Harbor. At much the same time (though the date was December 8 as it took place on the other side of the international date line), the Japanese also struck the Philippines, Hong Kong, and Malaya. On December 8, the United States declared war on Japan. Three days later, Germany and Italy declared war on the United States, and the American nation was deeply involved in World War II with major opponents on two widely separated fronts.

The United States entered the war at a time when Germany's position in Europe was very strong. In the U.S.S.R., the German armies, together with their north and central European allies, had driven deep into the western part of the country. They were at the very gates of Moscow when they were halted by the onset of a winter which was harsh even by Russian standards, and a revival of Soviet military strength. In North Africa, German and Italian forces were involved in a seesaw campaign along the coast with the British 8th Army, but were generally in the ascendant. And in the Atlantic, German U-boats continued to decimate the convoys bringing food, fuel, raw materials, and weapons to the United Kingdom.

American leaders had already given considerable thought to the progress of the war. In the short term and well before the United States could bring its growing strength to bear, it seemed likely that Germany would defeat the U.S.S.R. This was a grim prospect, for it opened the possibility of a German move to the west in huge strength, launching its own forces from the springboard provided by the manpower, raw materials, and industries of the areas Germany had already conquered.

During the summer of 1941, army and navy leaders had responded to a presidential request with the Victory Program, a refined version of the "Rainbow 5" plan. German ambitions were to be checked by bombing, blockade, subversion, and limited offensives, while the United States gathered its strength for an invasion of Europe followed by the defeat of Germany on its own ground. During this period, Japan's ambitions would be contained by American air and sea power, Chinese manpower, and the eastern armies of the U.S.S.R. Only after Germany had been crushed would the full weight of American strength be turned against Japan, which was then expected to crumble swiftly into defeat.

Opposite: Devastation after the Japanese attack on Pearl Harbor. This was the scene in the flooded Dry Dock No.1, which held three ships. In the foreground are the destroyers U.S.S. *Cassin* (right) and U.S.S. *Downes* (left), which were both severely damaged. In the background is the battleship U.S.S. *Pennsylvania*, which was badly but not severely damaged. The *Cassin* and *Downes*, both sister-ships of the *Shaw* were so badly damaged that their machinery and armament were removed and installed in two new hulls launched at the Mare Island Navy Yard in the middle of 1943 and later commissioned with the same names.

The Victory Program

The United Kingdom was a key component in this plan, both as an ally and as a springboard for operations in Europe. American planners were aware that the British were already weary after two years of war and had only limited resources. They concluded therefore that the United States would have to produce most of the western Allies' weapons and also supply a large proportion of the necessary manpower. The army now proposed 154 infantry divisions, 61 armored divisions, and 239 combat air groups. With support elements, this first-line strength demanded an army of 8,800,000 men, including 5,000,000 for deployment against Germany.

Yet the Victory Program reflected the views of the military establishment, not of national policy, which was still concerned to a large extent with hemisphere defense. During the time that the Victory Program was being prepared, American mobilization and rearmament were actually slowing down in line with the popular and political belief that American involvement would not mean raising and committing huge armies, but rather creating and using a small army as part of an American effort whose major features would be air and naval power and a massive industrial effort.

Pearl Harbor destroyed all such illusions, which had been based on hope, rather than the belief that the United States might still be able to avoid any entanglement in overseas wars. Politicians and the public had responded apathetically to the German attacks on the two destroyers, but it was now clear

Right: The scene at Battleship Row in Pearl Harbor only seconds before the attack that was to sink four battleships and critically damage two more within 40 minutes of the first strike.

Ernest J. King
For further references
see pages
29, 34, 43

that a huge war effort was needed. In January 1942, President Roosevelt proclaimed fresh goals: aircraft production of 60,000 in 1942 rising to 125,000 in 1943, tank production of 45,000 in 1942 rising to 75,000 in 1943, anti-aircraft gun production of 20,000 in 1942 rising to 35,000 in 1943, machine-gun production of 500,000 in 1942 rising to 1,000,000 in 1943, and merchant shipping production of 8,000,000 tons in 1942 rising to 10,000,000 tons in 1943.

At the same time, the administration admitted that the United States could not avoid the commitment of major ground forces, and the army began to plan for an overall strength of 10,000,000 men, starting with 3,600,000 by the end of 1942 as the personnel for 71 divisions and 115 combat aircraft groups plus support elements.

Admiral Ernest J. King was the Chief of Naval Operations through most of World War II. He was bound by the overall policy of "Germany first," but was a keen advocate of major offensive operations against Japan in the Pacific.

The Arcadia Conference

Between December 22, 1941, and January 14, 1942, Roosevelt and Churchill met in the so-called Arcadia Conference in Washington, D.C. Together with their senior military advisers, the two statesmen planned the overall structure for the Allied conduct of the war. They were faced with a difficult decision; in the eastern theater, the Japanese were making startling progress against the Americans and British, while in the western theater, the collapse of the U.S.S.R. seemed imminent. Roosevelt and Churchill nevertheless decided to stick to the "Germany first" policy that had already been formulated. They appreciated that the defeat of "Fortress Germany" could not be achieved quickly or easily. Therefore, 1942 would see mainly defensive and preparatory work, together with limited offensives should the opportunity arise. 1943 would, in all probability, see an Allied return to the European mainland.

The Arcadia Conference also decided that there should be complete unity of command in each theater and set up the Combined Chiefs of Staff. The CCS was a committee whose members were the professional military leaders of both countries. It was responsible to the president and prime minister and had the task of planning and controlling the coalition's grand strategy. The American members of the CCS were General Marshall (Army Chief of Staff), Admiral Harold R. Stark (Chief of Naval Operations), who was replaced early in 1942 by Admiral Ernest J. King, and Lieutenant General Henry H. Arnold (Chief and later Commanding General of the Army Air Forces). In July 1942 a fourth American, Admiral William D. Leahy, the president's chief of staff, was added. The CCS was based in Washington, and since its British members could attend only infrequently, they were usually represented by the four senior members of the British Joint Senior Staff Mission in Washington. The CCS inevitably sprouted a system of subcommittees to deal with specific matters such as transportation, logistics, and communications.

The Joint Chiefs of Staff Committee

A similar, though unchartered, organization for the control of the country's military affairs was the Joint Chiefs of Staff. By February 1942, this body had emerged as the highest American military authority, with direct responsibility to the president. The JCS was made up of the four American members of the CCS. Like the CCS, it soon developed a network of subordinate bodies, including the Joint Staff Planners, the Joint Strategic Survey Committee, and the Joint Logistics Committee.

In the spring of 1942, the Americans and the British finalized arrangements for a worldwide division of strategic leadership. The American JCS was responsible for the war in the Pacific; the British JCS was responsible for the war in the Middle East and Indian Ocean. Combined responsibility would be exercised for the war in the Atlantic, western Europe, and the Mediterranean. China was designated a separate theater under the Nationalist Chinese leader, Chiang Kai-shek. In the Pacific, the American JCS created two main strategic theaters, namely the Southwest Pacific Area under MacArthur, and the Pacific Ocean Areas under Admiral Chester W. Nimitz. The latter was divided into the North, Central, and South Pacific Areas, with the first two controlled directly by Nimitz and the last by Admiral William F. Halsey, Jr., Nimitz's next-in-command. This eastern theater arrangement was modified later in 1942 by the creation of the U.S. Army Forces, China-Burma-India, under Lieutenant General Joseph W. Stilwell, who was Chiang Kai-shek's chief of staff.

General Staff Problems

The General Staff in the War Department had grown considerably from the size and responsibility it had possessed from 1921. Designed for coordination and planning, it was now a large operating organization whose most important subdivisions were the War Plans and Supply Divisions. The effects of this growth in size were an increase in the burden of responsibility placed on the Chief of Staff, and a reduction in policy making and planning as the General Staff's officers became immersed in day-to-day detail. Three other features of the General Staff required modification. First was the continued control of the Army Air Forces by the General Staff at a time when the unit wanted autonomy. Second was the odd position of the General Headquarters, whose responsibilities in field command and training overlapped with those of the General Staff in many areas. Third was the division of responsibility for supply between the Supply Division, which looked after requirements and distribution, and the Office of the Under Secretary of War, which was responsible for procurement.

General Henry H. ("Hap") Arnold started the war as Chief of the Army Air Force and later became Commanding General of the Army Air Forces. With Marshall and King, he was one of the U.S. service leaders on the Anglo-American Combined Chiefs of Staff and favored the strategic bombing policy.

George C. Marshall

For further references
see pages
14, *15*, *29*, 34, 43, 71, 97

Loading a Bofors gun. In common with most other countries, the United States had in the 1930s underestimated the capabilities of tactical air power, and she therefore lacked adequate short-range antiaircraft artillery when the country was drawn into World War II. Like other countries, though, the United States found one highly effective solution. The government licensed production of a Swedish weapon, the 40-mm Bofors gun, that offered a powerful projectile, moderately high rate of fire, accuracy, and the right combination of high traverse and elevation speeds for easy tracking of target aircraft. The type was standardized in April 1941, but deliveries of the 40-mm Light Antiaircraft Gun M1 began only in 1943. Thereafter the weapon was produced in very large numbers.

Marshall's Reorganization

On March 9, 1942, General Marshall implemented a thorough reorganization of the War Department. The General Staff was reduced in size and responsibility, although the War Plans and Intelligence Divisions were maintained to allow GS to concentrate on its original tasks of war planning and policy guidance. The War Plans Division was expanded and later renamed the Operations Division. It became Marshall's command post and, as such, was the agency which directed the conduct of the war overseas. The Army Air Forces were allocated almost complete control of aircraft procurement, personnel, training, and operational doctrine at both the tactical and strategic levels. The reorganization also created two new commands, the Army Ground Forces and the Services of Supply. The Army Ground Forces, under Lieutenant General Lesley J. McNair, assumed the training role of the discontinued General Headquarters and absorbed the various ground combat arms. The Services of Supply were later

Major, 101st Airborne Division, 1944

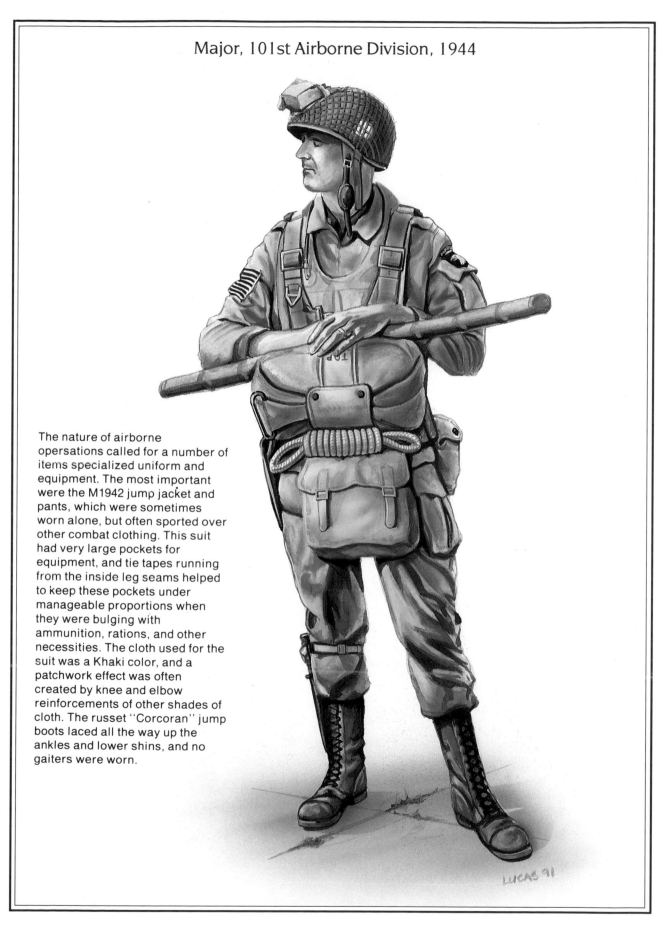

The nature of airborne opersations called for a number of items specialized uniform and equipment. The most important were the M1942 jump jacket and pants, which were sometimes worn alone, but often sported over other combat clothing. This suit had very large pockets for equipment, and tie tapes running from the inside leg seams helped to keep these pockets under manageable proportions when they were bulging with ammunition, rations, and other necessities. The cloth used for the suit was a Khaki color, and a patchwork effect was often created by knee and elbow reinforcements of other shades of cloth. The russet ''Corcoran'' jump boots laced all the way up the ankles and lower shins, and no gaiters were worn.

U-Boats
For further references
see pages
19, 21, 24, *33*, 127, *131*

The backbone of the German U-boat arm was provided in the first part of World War II by "Type VII" class submarines such as the *U-101*. Displacing 753 tons surfaced and 857 tons submerged, these 44-man boats were 218 feet 3 inches long and carried an armament of one 88-mm gun, one 20-mm cannon, and five 533-mm torpedo tubes (four forward and one aft) with 12 torpedoes or 14 mines. Power was provided by a diesel motor delivering a surface speed of 17·25 knots, and an electric motor with a submerged speed of 8 knots. Range was 6,500 miles at 12 knots on the surface, and 80 miles at 4 knots submerged. The *U-101* was built by Germania Werft at Kiel and launched in February 1940. By 1943, the boat was obsolete and was paid off in November of that year.

renamed the Army Service Forces and, under the command of Lieutenant General Brehon B. Somervell, controlled the supply and administrative services, the nine corps areas, and most of the army posts in the United States.

On December 7, 1941, the United States had been rearming steadily for more than 18 months. Yet it was still poorly prepared for war. The army numbered 1,644,000 men organized into four armies, 37 divisions (30 infantry, five armored, and two cavalry), and more than 40 combat air groups. Two of the divisions were in Hawaii and one in the Philippines, and some 200,000 more men were in other overseas garrisons. This left a notional 17 divisions in the U.S. to deal with an invasion, but these forces were still poorly equipped, especially in heavy and high-technology weapons. They were also woefully short of ammunition. In fact, this shortage was so severe, that the army was not prepared to commit more than one division and one anti aircraft regiment to any theater where combat seemed imminent. This meant that up to April 1942, the army was able to send only a single division-size task force to the hard-pressed Pacific theater.

Slow Growth in Strength

Slowly the position began to improve as further enlistment and training strengthened the forces. Industrial production increased, and a certain amount of Lend-Lease equipment was diverted to American units. By April, the army had 13 divisions virtually ready to move overseas. The destination for these forces was mainly the United Kingdom, but transportation was a problem.

Shipping was available, but protection against the U-boats was almost totally lacking. The period between January and April 1942 was known to the crews of the U-boats as the second "happy time" of their war. Soon after Germany's declaration of war, the U-boats were sent to operate off the American east coast. The sea lanes there were virtually unprotected, and potential targets were silhouetted against the lights of brightly lit coastal towns and cities. In the first four

In the early stages of the fight against U-boats operating in the western Atlantic, the most effective land-based patrol plane was the Consolidated Liberator. The first Liberator produced in truly mass production numbers was the B-24D bomber. Many of them were operated on deep-ocean patrols, where their range and offensive armament proved important and perhaps decisive. The U.S. Navy operated a similar model, the PB4Y-1, in the same role.

months of the year, the U-boats sank 80 American merchant ships without the slightest difficulty except for the range at which they were operating from their bases. Even this difficulty was eased when the first "milch cow" submarines arrived on the scene. These supply craft carried fuel oil, torpedoes, and food and could reprovision operational boats at sea. The U-boats could therefore extend their endurance on patrol as they took maximum advantage of the American lack of preparedness.

The U-boats' "Happy Time"

In December 1941, the U.S. Navy had only 20 surface vessels and perhaps 100 aircraft to protect the eastern seaboard. During the winter, this pitifully small force had been bolstered by army aircraft, armed British trawlers, and many improvised craft. Finally in the late spring of 1942, the situation on the east coast began to ease with the introduction of an effective convoy system and the hard-won experience of the escort forces. Between May and August, the task of the U-boats

on the United States' eastern coast became increasingly difficult. During this period, the German captains increasingly switched their attentions to the north and south, venturing as far north as the mouth of the St. Lawrence River in Canada and as far south as the estuary of the Orinoco River in Venezuela. This gave the American planners the chance to organize the movement of large ground forces into the United Kingdom.

A cornerstone of American and British planning at the time was the need to keep the U.S.S.R. in the war by drawing off German forces to the west. This strategy demanded the opening of a "second front" in Europe as early as possible. The Americans and the British agreed that the United Kingdom should be the springboard for this "second front," but disagreed on virtually everything else, such as timing and invasion area. The American JCS wanted to launch an invasion of northwestern Europe as soon as possible, but the British JCS and Prime Minister Churchill feared that such a move would be premature and suffer a catastrophic failure against a German war machine at the height of its powers. The

British therefore preferred an indirect approach, through the "soft underbelly" of the Mediterranean.

Coalition Planning

The CCS deliberations were long and difficult. The U.S. wanted a decisive blow to help the U.S.S.R. as early as possible. A tentative decision was made to launch Operation "Round-up," a major landing in Europe during the spring of 1943. However, if the U.S.S.R. appeared to be on the verge of collapse, Operation "Sledgehammer" would be launched against the Cherbourg peninsula in France at any time up to the fall of 1942, using whatever forces were on hand, mainly British.

Movement of U.S. troops to the United Kingdom began in June 1942, with the intention of building up a force of more than a million American fighting men for "Round-up." The whole program was then thrown into disarray by British reverses in North Africa, where the success of Axis forces was threatening the British position in Egypt. Shipping had to be diverted to take additional men and weapons to the forces in Egypt via the long route around the Cape of Good Hope. So, by August 1942, only about 170,000 American soldiers had reached the United Kingdom. Since the British were slated to provide more than half the transportation for U.S. soldiers across the Atlantic, it soon became clear that the shipping shortage was making "Round-up" logistically impossible for the planned time in 1943. Both sides remained fully committed to the concept of an invasion of northwestern Europe, but now saw the plan as a longer-term objective and agreed to cancel "Sledgehammer," even as an emergency measure.

At this time, the British proposed, even more strongly, a venture that they had already broached at the Arcadia Conference. It was an operation which would get American troops into useful combat, but at considerably less risk than the planned European landing. This was Operation "Torch," an amphibious descent on the French colonies in Northwest Africa. The British argued that the seizure of Morocco and Algeria, followed by an advance into Tunisia, would trap the Axis forces facing the British on the Egyptian/Libyan frontier between two Allied armies. In the long run, the plan would provide the Allies with an ideal base for further offensive operations and bring more French forces into the war. It would also save enormous amounts of Allied shipping by opening the route through the Mediterranean and Suez Canal as an alternative to the long haul around the Cape of Good Hope. Churchill did not at this stage mention his longer-term objective: the use of North Africa as the springboard for an invasion of southern Europe.

American Fears

Stimson, Marshall, King, and Arnold were deeply opposed to the plan. They feared the consequences of defeat, but feared the consequences of victory almost as much. Victory, they thought, would almost inevitably lead to continued operations around the southern edge of Europe, which they felt was wholly opposed to their strategic ideal of concentrating mass and effort against the main enemy by the most direct approach.

Ironically, the British found that their main ally for an operation in Northwest Africa was Roosevelt, who was determined to get American ground forces into combat in the western theater before the end of 1942. The president therefore decided in favor of the British plan during July 1942 and effectively killed any possibility of an Allied invasion of northwestern Europe in 1943.

In August 1943, the CCS decided that the Commander, Allied Expeditionary Force, would be an American officer. Lieutenant General Dwight D. Eisenhower, currently commanding the U.S. forces in the United Kingdom, was chosen for the position, and he selected his subordinates in the Allied Force Headquarters on the basis of competence regardless of nationality. The considerable disagreement between the two parties covered such fundamentals as the landing points. The American view was to restrict these sites to the Atlantic coast of Morocco to make any Spanish or German intervention more difficult, while the British wanted landings on the Mediterranean coast of Algeria to make an eastward move into Tunisia easier. The result was a compromise that included both options.

The task of the planners was made all the more difficult by the three-faction nature of the administration in French North Africa. Secret negotiations undertaken in an effort to reduce the chance of the landings being opposed were not completely successful.

Operation "Torch"

In its final form, "Torch" comprised three groups of landings by three separate task forces. The Western Task Force, under Major General George S. Patton, Jr., sailed directly from ports on the east coast. Escorted by a U.S. Navy squadron commanded by Rear Admiral Henry K. Hewitt, the force included 35,000 fighting troops in 39 ships. The Central and Eastern Task Forces sailed from British ports under escort of Royal Navy warships. The Central Task Force had 39,000 American soldiers in 49 ships and was commanded by Major General Lloyd R. Fredendall, while the Eastern Task Force under Major General Charles W. Ryder had 33,000 American and British troops in 34 ships.

The Western Task Force was to land on Morocco's Atlantic coast, and the Central and Eastern Task Forces were to come ashore on Algeria's Mediterranean coast. In overall terms, the Allied plan called for the two American groups to consolidate in Morocco and Algeria to deal with any German and Spanish intervention, while the British elements of the Eastern Task Force moved east toward Tunisia. They would be the leading wave of the British 1st Army to be established in northwestern Africa.

The three task groups arrived off their invasion areas during the night of November 7/8, and the landings went in during the early morning of November 8 at times dictated by the tide. The operational plan for each task force was basically similar: landings were to be made on each

Left: Although he started the war as a comparatively junior divisional commander, George S. Patton, Jr., rose rapidly to high command (the 7th Army in the Sicilian campaign and the 3rd Army in the Northwest European campaign) and emerged from the war as one of the nation's most celebrated generals.

Below: Another comparatively junior commander who rose even more rapidly to high command was Dwight D. Eisenhower, who in 1945 controlled all the Allied armies fighting the Germans.

side of a major city and port. This area would then be pinched off together with local airfields, so that harbor facilities and landing sites for aircraft would become available as early in the consolidation as possible.

The United States Enters Combat

The Western Task Force landed in three areas. At Safi, 125 miles southwest of Casablanca, the 47th Regimental Combat Team of the 9th Infantry Division and Combat Command B of the 2nd Armored Division under Major General Ernest Harmon encountered determined resistance from French colonial troops, but secured their beachhead. They then moved off toward Casablanca before halting at Mazagan when the news of a French ceasefire was announced.

At Fedala, 15 miles northeast of Casablanca, the reinforced 3rd Infantry Division landed against very determined opposition. That resistance was eventually silenced with the aid of naval gunfire, allowing the division to make for Casablanca. At Port Lyautey, about 25 miles farther to the northeast, the reinforced 60th RCT of Major General Lucien K. Truscott's 9th Infantry Division took the city and airfield in two days of

hard fighting, again with admirable support from naval vessels. The French commander in Casablanca refused to consider surrender for two days, but then ordered his forces in Morocco to offer no further resistance.

The Axis powers knew that the convoys carrying the Central and Western Task Forces had sailed into the Mediterranean on November 5/6. They thought, however, that their destinations lay far to the east and planned to tackle them closer to Italian air and naval bases. The Central Task Force began to put its men ashore very early on November 8. Rangers quickly silenced the gun batteries at Arzeu, northeast of Oran, and the 16th, 18th, and 26th RCTs of the 1st Infantry Division took Arzeu and Les Andalouses, the latter lying west of Oran. This allowed the two armored task forces of the 1st Armored Division's Combat Command B to take the airfields at Lourmel and Tafaraqui without difficulty. The latter had been the objective of the 2nd Battalion, 509th Parachute Infantry Regiment, but this force had landed well to the west of its target on the Sebkra, a dried salt lake, and reached the airfield after the tanks. The last component of the Oran operation was the attempt by two U.S. Coast Guard cutters to land an assault party in Oran harbor, but the ships were detected

Operation "Torch" brought U.S. ground forces into action against the Germans and Italians for the first time. The action played a decisive part in bringing the war in North Africa to a successful conclusion for the Allies.

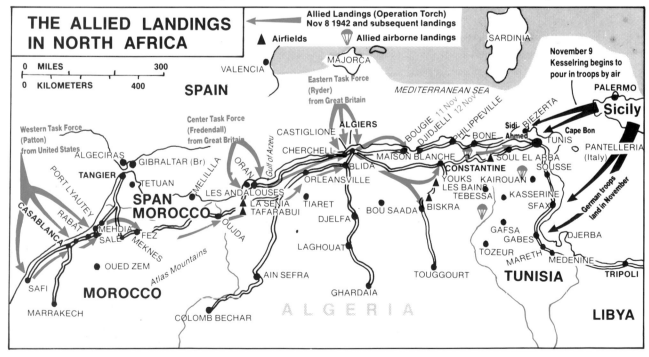

THE ALLIED LANDINGS IN NORTH AFRICA

Allied Landings (Operation Torch) Nov 8 1942 and subsequent landings
▲ Airfields   Allied airborne landings

Adolf Hitler

For further references
see pages
8, 48, 69, 79, 84, 86, 90,
91, 94, 96, 111, 116, 122

George S. Patton

For further references
see pages
35, 41, 42, 44, 45, 48, 49,
50, 92, 93, 95, 96, 102,
109, 116, 117, 120

Major General George
S. Patton, Jr., (with two
stars on his helmet) and
Rear Admiral J.L. Hall
(foreground) prepare
to land in French North
Africa during
Operation "Torch."

and heavily engaged, and the surviving men were forced to surrender. The Americans tightened their noose around Oran, and the French capitulated on November 10.

The Eastern Task Force encountered very little resistance, mainly because pro-Allied French units had seized the area around Algiers. Despite the repulse of another shipborne attempt to seize the harbor, British forces landed west of the city, and British commandos and the 39th RCT east of the city. They were already in position around the city when the Vichy French faction regained control during the morning, and by early evening, the British force had quelled all opposition. One of the French officers captured in Algiers was Admiral Jean Francois Darlan, the commander of the Vichy forces; and after delicate negotiations, he assumed full authority in North Africa and ordered a ceasefire.

A Rapid German Response

The immediate result of "Torch" for the Germans and French was a flurry of political and military activity as the Allies tried to win over the French political and military apparatus in North Africa. In the short term, Hitler ordered the creation of an airhead in Tunisia to hold this vital area for the Axis. He also commanded the forces in occupied France to move into unoccupied Vichy France while the Italians occupied Corsica. About a thousand German troops were arriving by air in Bizerte and Tunis each day, and the British were eager for a rapid advance to seize the area before the Germans consolidated their airhead, which would enable stronger Axis forces to arrive. British infantry was lifted by sea from Algiers to Bougie on November 11, and the following day, British commandos

When initial French resistance had ended, the transports were able to move closer inshore, which made the task of ferrying reinforcements and supplies to the beach near Oran in western Algeria much easier.

Erwin Rommel
For further references
see pages
39, 40,41, 79, 80, 84, 86

Jurgen von Arnim
For further references

and airborne forces arrived in Bone. The Allies wanted to secure key points at the eastern end of the Atlas Mountains and in the western Dorsal range, so between November 15 and 17 airborne forces were dropped to secure airfields and then move forward by land. The 2nd Battalion of the 509th Parachute Infantry Regiment dropped at Youks les Bains and then advanced via Tebessa to Gafsa.

Free French forces in Tunisia had meanwhile been pulling back from the German airhead and linked up with the Allied spearheads on November 17. From this date, the British 1st Army pushed its men forward as fast as possible; by November 28, this force was within 20 miles of Tunis, where it was checked, and in places pushed back, by determined German counterattacks. Bad weather on the 500-mile overland route from Tunis made it impossible for the Allies to sustain their momentum, and it was now clear that the Allies would have to fight for Tunisia.

Stalemate in the Mountains

The Axis forces held the northern part of the area, west of Bizerte and Tunis on a north/south line from Cape Serrat to Bou Arada, strongly, and farther south, patrols screened the line of the eastern Dorsal range as larger forces were built up around Sousse, Sfax, and Gabes. The British V Corps faced the main Axis strength, while the Axis forces in the eastern Dorsal were faced by Allied patrol units provided by the French in the center and the Americans in the south. As more troops arrived, the center of the Allied line was allocated to the French XIX Corps, and the south to Fredendall's U.S. II Corps, which included French as well as American units. II Corps' original task was an attack toward Sfax with the intention of cutting the Axis line of communications, which linked Colonel General Jurgen von Arnim's 5th Panzer Army in Tunisia with Field Marshal Erwin Rommel's German-Italian Panzer Army as it pulled backed through Cyrenaica and Tripolitania after its crushing defeat in the 2nd Battle of El Alamein. However, when Eisenhower learned that the British 8th Army expected to reach southern Tunisia only in mid-February 1943, II Corps' task was altered to defense of the eastern Dorsal range.

In January and the first part of 1943,

A World War I art that was revived and developed in World War II was camouflage. The primary objective was to prevent enemy reconnaissance aircraft from detecting ground forces which meant that major attacks could be launched with complete tactical surprise. Seen at short range from the ground, camouflage against aerial reconnaissance appears wholly inadequate, but the combination of a natural obstacle (the tree), the right tone of paint, and branches and netting would have been highly effective in breaking up this half-track carrier's outline.

von Arnim kept the Allies off balance with a series of probing attacks. Eisenhower decided to ease the command situation by subordinating the French XIX and U.S. II Corps to the British 1st Army. The French, notably weak in armor, were reinforced by Combat Command B of the U.S. 1st Armored Division. This move left Fredendall with the 1st Infantry Division and the rest of the 1st Armored Division, which now included Combat Commands A and C, supported by the provisional Combat Command D. By the middle of February, II Corps was in poor tactical shape, with its formations divided and intermingled. At this point, Rommel prepared to join von Arnim in an attack on the corps.

Rommel's suggestion was a dual offensive by the 10th and 21st Panzer Divisions of the 5th Panzer Army, and the German Africa Corps of the German-Italian Panzer Army. The 5th Panzer Army detachment was to take Sidi Bou Zid and move on Sbeitla, while the German Africa Corps was to take Gafsa and drive on Feriana. At this point, the 21st Panzer Division was to be detached to the German Africa Corps. This combined force would cap-ture Kasserine and undertake an offensive through the western Dorsal via the Kasserine Pass, which could then be exploited for the capture of the Allied base at Tebessa.

The Germans Counterattack

The 10th and 21st Panzer Divisions attacked on February 14 and secured immediate success against Combat Command A of Major General Orlando Ward's 1st Armored Division, with the 168th RCT attached. The 168th RCT was cut off, and only a few men escaped when a breakout was attempted on February 17. At the same time, CCA pulled back with heavy losses in the face of strong armored thrusts with effective dive-bomber and ground-attack air support. Ward underestimated the German strength and planned a counterattack by CCC, reinforced by a battalion of CCA. The counterattack was a disaster: one battalion was virtually destroyed, and the others escaped only with heavy losses.

The British 1st Army now released the rest of CCB to Ward and ordered Freden-

Albert Kesselring
For further references
see pages
52, 54, 56, 61, 62, 64,
66, 69

dall to pull II Corps back to the western Dorsal while maintaining forward positions in Sbeitla, Kasserine, and Feriana. By the evening of February 16, the 1st Armored Division was concentrating at Sbeitla.

The German Africa Corps had attacked on February 15. This southern part of the German pincer had passed through Gafsa on the same day and was now making good progress to Feriana, which was captured on February 17. Von Arnim decided that Rommel did not now need the 21st Panzer Division and ordered his two Panzer divisions to destroy Sbeitla before advancing northeast on Fondouk. The 1st Armored Division barely managed to avoid a panic-struck rout in its first night battle, but covered by CCB, it fought its way clear and pulled back to Tebessa, with other units covering the Kasserine and Sbiba passes.

Rommel was now sure that a fast offensive north through Tebessa toward the sea at Bone would force the Allies to pull back or face the prospect of being cut off. Von Arnim refused to provide the support necessary for such a move, and it was only after Rommel had approached von Arnim's superior, Field Marshal Albert Kesselring, that he was given overall command. However, because the axis of Rommel's offensive passed through the Italian command structure nominally controlling North African operations, the focus was changed from Tebessa to Thala and Sbiba. On February 19, Rommel ordered attacks through the Kasserine and Sbiba passes. Intending to exploit the more successful of the two, he recalled the 10th Panzer Division from its advance against Fondouk to become part of the drive through the Kasserine Pass.

The Battle of Kasserine Pass

Neither offensive achieved any real success on February 19, and though the fighting continued until February 22, the Germans made only slow progress. The 21st Panzer Division was checked in the

U.S. infantry advances past a German tank destroyed in the fighting for Kasserine Pass in southern Tunisia.

American armored and infantry units received an unexpectedly rough handling by the experienced German formations and their proven equipment in the Tunisian fighting. Examining captured or destroyed German tanks, in places such as this equipment graveyard in Tunisia could provide useful information about enemy strengths and weaknesses.

Harold Alexander
For further references
see pages
41, 44, 49, 57, 62, 63,
64, 65, 66, 67, 69, 70

Sbiba thrust by British armor, supported by the artillery of the 9th Infantry Division, and in the Kasserine Pass, the German Africa Corps and 10th Panzer Division were halted by CCB and the 1st Infantry Division. Rommel called off the operation during February 22 and began to withdraw his forces without interference from the Allies. The Allies regained Kasserine on February 25, ending a small but important battle that had cost the Germans only 2,000 casualties to the Allies' 10,000, including 6,500 in II Corps.

On February 23, Rommel was appointed overall commander of what now became Army Group "Africa," controlling the 5th Panzer Army in the north and the German-Italian 1st Army (previously the German-Italian Panzer Army) in the south. If this appointment had been made just two weeks earlier, the battle might very well have gone the other way.

Allied Revisions

The battle had serious implications for the Allies, for it had revealed a number of deficiencies: a complex command structure, the problems of mixing units of more than one nationality in any formation, and the unwieldiness of the American close support air tactics. Among the Allied moves were the creation of General the Hon. Sir Harold Alexander's 18th Army Group to head all operations in Africa, the creation of single-nationality operational sectors, the adoption of British air support tactics by the U.S. forces, and Patton's appointment on March 6 to replace Fredendall as commander of II Corps.

The 18th Army Group decided that II Corps (1st, 9th, and 34th Infantry Divisions plus the 1st Armored Division) needed to revive its morale and sharpen its skills in a secondary operation before being entrusted with any major role. The tasks were the recapture of Gafsa as a supply center and a reconnaissance in force toward Maknassy. Patton wanted to drive to the coast, thereby cutting the Axis forces in two, but was specifically instructed not to exceed his orders for the attack between March 17 and 23. This assault achieved what was demanded of it and, by threatening communications between the 5th Panzer and 1st Armies, worried von Arnim so much that he ordered a counterattack by the 10th Panzer Division. The Germans were easily repulsed by the 1st Infantry Division on March 23, and as a result the 9th and 34th Divisions were released to Patton, who was ordered to advance to the coast east of Fondouk and El Guettar.

This drive was checked by the Axis forces, allowing the 1st Army to fall back to the north when its Mareth Line position was outflanked by the British 8th Army on March 27. By April 7, the British 8th Army had linked up with the right-hand elements of II Corps, but the Axis forces had escaped a possible trap.

An Aggressive Role

At Eisenhower's strong suggestion, II Corps was now given a more aggressive role and exchanged places with the British V Corps. Patton had to start work on plans for an invasion of Sicily and was replaced as II Corps' commander by Major General Omar N. Bradley on April 15, just one day before the corps completed its move to the

Allied left wing between the Mediterranean coast and Beja.

The Axis forces were now penned in a comparatively small area of northeastern Tunisia, centered on Bizerte and Tunis. The Allied plan for the final reduction of this position gave the main task — a central drive on Tunis — to the British V and IX Corps of the British 1st Army, with supporting roles on the flanks played by II Corps in the north and the British 8th Army (supported by the French XIX Corps that linked the British 1st and 8th Armies) in the south.

Preliminary operations were undertaken from April 22 to improve the Allies' basic positions. Facing the strongest opposition in the center and south, the British achieved only modest results. In the north, however, II Corps was faced by weaker forces and made comparatively good progress, despite the very difficult terrain. The Battle of Tunisia was fought

Omar N. Bradley
For further references see pages
42, 49, 73, 87, 89, 92, 95, 102, 108, 111, 115, 116

After the May 1943 victory in Tunisia, which finally expelled the Germans and Italians from North Africa, the Allies organized a victory parade in Tunis. More than 27,000 men took part.

between May 3 and 13. The Axis forces had no effective air support, no reserves, and precious little room to maneuver: as a result, they were driven steadily back. II Corps captured Bizerte on May 7 and linked up with British forces at Protville on May 8.

The End in Africa

The North African campaign ended on May 13 when 275,000 Axis soldiers surrendered. United States soldiers had been blooded in modern combat against high-quality opposition and had begun to emerge as an effective fighting force. American casualties between the launching of ''Torch'' and the Tunisian surrender had been about 18,500.

As these last events were unfolding, Allied planners were hard at work on the invasion of Sicily, which had been decided as the next objective of the Allied forces in North Africa during the Casablanca Conference. The United States had held out again for a scaling-down of Mediter-

ranean operations to speed the build-up of forces in the United Kingdom for an invasion of France later in 1943. When it became clear that the defeat of the Axis forces in Tunisia would come too late for an invasion of France to be feasible in 1943, Marshall and King suggested that the available Allied strength should not be used for a secondary campaign in the Mediterranean, but to help the Allies seize the initiative in the Pacific. The inevitable result was a compromise for limited operations in both the Pacific and the Mediterranean.

Sicily: An End, Not a Beginning

The United States was unhappy with this decision, but demanded that the Sicilian operation should be an end in itself and not the start of the ''soft underbelly'' option which was favored by the British. This strategy was feared by the United States as an open drain of men, weapons, and equipment that should be reserved for the main blow against Germany across

U.S. paratroopers make their final checks before leaving for the invasion of Sicily.

the English Channel. The Sicilian invasion became Operation "Husky," whose four objectives were to secure Allied communications through the Mediterranean, divert German strength from the U.S.S.R., apply pressure on Italy, and create the "situation in which Turkey can be enlisted as an active Ally."

Planning for "Husky" was slow because so many commanders were involved in the Tunisian operations, and it was only on May 3 that the invasion plans were finalized. The date chosen was May 10, because it offered the right tide and moon for a night assault by amphibious and airborne forces.

The decision about the actual invasion points had to take account of the Allies' need to seize or capture ports and airfields as early in the campaign as possible. It was therefore decided initially that the British 8th Army would land on the southeastern coast, and that two and five days later, Lieutenant General

Patton's new 7th Army would land near Marsala and Palermo respectively. The idea behind the staggered times was to allow captured airfields to be brought into operation for each successive landing.

An Allied Disagreement

The British objected that the plan dispersed the Allied strength too widely and did not allow for the early capture of enough airfields. In addition, Eisenhower was worried that too much reliance was being placed on resupply over the beaches rather than through captured ports, and finally he fixed on a different plan.

To distract the attention of the Axis powers, naval diversions were to be made against the western tip of Sicily and western Greece. Then Alexander's 15th Army Group, the 7th and British 8th Armies, would land in southern Sicily, with the

The main weight of the American strategic air offensive in Europe was carried by the Boeing B-17 Flying Fortress. The definitive version of this high-altitude bomber was the B-17G. Derived from the B-17F, it had improved defensive armament, including a twin-gun chin turret to meet the head-on attacks developed by German fighter pilots to attack the B-17F. These B-17Gs belonged to the 532nd Bombardment Squadron, one of the four squadrons that made up the 8th Army Air Force's 381st Bombardment Group.

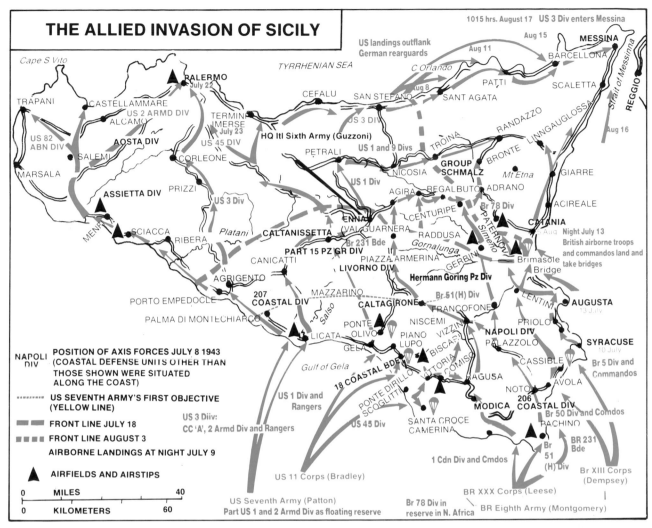

THE ALLIED INVASION OF SICILY

1015 hrs. August 17 US 3 Div enters Messina

US landings outflank
German rearguards

Aug 15

TYRRHENIAN SEA

Aug 11

MESSINA

BARCELLONA

Cape S Vito

C Orlando

PATTI

SCALETTA

Strait of Messina

TRAPANI

CASTELLAMMARE

CEFALU

Aug 8

SAN STEFANO

SANT AGATA

REGGIO

US 2 ARMD DIV

US 3 DIV

RANDAZZO

Aug 16

ALCAMO

TERMINI
IMERSE
July 23

HQ Itl Sixth Army (Guzzoni)

TROINA

LINNGAUGLOSSA

US 82
ABN DIV

SALEMI

AOSTA DIV

US 45 DIV

PETRALI

US 1 and 9 Divs

BRONTE

GIARRE

MARSALA

CORLEONE

GROUP
SCHMALZ

Mt Etna

ACIREALE

PRIZZI

US 1 Div

NICOSIA

ASSIETTA DIV

US 3 DIV

AGIRA

REGALBUTO ADRANO

SCIACCA

RIBERA

Platani

CALTANISSETTA

ENNA
(VALGUARNERA)

CENTURIPE

Br 78 Div

CATANIA

PATERNO

5 Aug

MENFI

Br 231 Bde

RADDUSA

Simeto

Night July 13
British airborne troops
and commandos land and
take bridges

PART 15 PZ GR DIV

Gornalunga

CANICATTI

PIAZZA ARMERINA

GERBINI

Brimasole
Bridge

PORTO EMPEDOCLE

LIVORNO DIV

Hermann Goring Pz Div

PALMA DI MONTECHIARCO

MAZZARINO

Salso

207
COASTAL DIV

CALTAGIRONE

Br 51(H) Div

LENTINI

FRANCOFONE

AUGUSTA

AGRIGENTO

PONTE
OLIVO

NISCEMI

NAPOLI DIV

PRIOLO

13 July

LICATA

PIANO
LUPO

VIZZINI

PALAZZOLO

SYRACUSE

GELA

BISCARI

CASSIBLE

10 July

Gulf of Gela

18 COASTAL BDE

COMISO

VITTORIA

RAGUSA

Br 5 Div and
Commandos

US 1 Div and
Rangers

PONTE DIRILLO
SCOGLITTI

SANTA CROCE
CAMERINA

MODICA

NOTO

AVOLA

206
COASTAL DIV

Br 50 Div and Comdos

US 45 Div

PACHINO

BR 231
Bde

1 Cdn Div and Cmdos

Br
51
(H) Div

Br XIII Corps
(Dempsey)

Legend

NAPOLI DIV POSITION OF AXIS FORCES JULY 8 1943
(COASTAL DEFENSE UNITS OTHER THAN
THOSE SHOWN WERE SITUATED
ALONG THE COAST)

········ US SEVENTH ARMY'S FIRST OBJECTIVE
(YELLOW LINE)

▬ ▬ FRONT LINE JULY 18

■ ■ FRONT LINE AUGUST 3

AIRBORNE LANDINGS AT NIGHT JULY 9

▲ AIRFIELDS AND AIRSTIPS

US 3 Div:
CC 'A', 2 Armd Div and Rangers

0 MILES 40

0 KILOMETERS 60

US 11 Corps (Bradley)

US Seventh Army (Patton)
Part US 1 and 2 Armd Div as floating reserve

Br 78 Div in
reserve in N. Africa

BR XXX Corps (Leese)

BR Eighth Army (Montgomery)

British mainly on the southeastern coast and the Americans on the southwestern coast.

As soon as the Tunisian campaign was over, the Allied air forces began to prepare the way for "Husky" with a campaign against Axis air strength in the Italian theater. The islands of Lampedusa, Linosa, and Pantelleria were deluged with bombs and then captured by amphibious assault, while air bases in Sardinia, Sicily, and southern Italy were devastated by a campaign undertaken by the Allies' medium and heavy bomber fleets during the month before the scheduled landings. So, on the eve of "Husky," the Axis forces could count on the support of only 1,300 aircraft (including 600 obsolescent Italian machines) to the Allies 3,680.

As Axis air strength was being decimated, the commanders completed their preparations. The 7th Army was mustered, trained, and embarked in ports and adjoining areas between Bizerte and Algiers, while the British 8th Army was gathered between Sfax and ports in Syria. Most of the formations earmarked for "Husky" had previously seen combat in North Africa, but some fresh divisions also arrived from the United States and the United Kingdom, raising Allied strength to 478,000 against the 365,000 men available to the Italian 6th Army in Sicily.

Operation "Husky"

The overall plan called for the use of airborne forces to take major objectives that would facilitate the consolidation of the first beachheads, the seizure of two ports (Licata and Syracuse), and the capture of airfields in southern Sicily. The

U.S. and British forces became partners again for Operation "Hugo." This landing in Sicily confirmed Patton as one of the greatest commanders of the war.

Taken by a cameraman on the aircraft carrier U.S.S. *Yorktown* at Norfolk Navy Station on June 22, 1943, this photograph shows the U.S.S. *Vulcan* departing for the Mediterranean. This repair ship was one of the many service vessels doing invaluable work in keeping warships operational in distant waters. The *Vulcan*, one of a four-ship class, displaced 9,140 tons. The ship carried an armament of four 5-inch and eight 40-mm guns, a mass of support equipment and spare parts, and a large number of highly skilled technicians and repair specialists among a 1,297-man crew.

WORLD WAR II – THE WAR IN EUROPE

two armies could then combine along a line from Pozzallo to Vizzini via Ragusa. With this southern corner of the island in their hands, the Allies would then drive north with the emphasis on the right, where the ports of Augusta and Catania were to be captured, together with the complex of airfields around Gerbini. Only then would the methodical reduction of the rest of the island be contemplated.

Because of the weather conditions, the airborne landings were in general unsuccessful, and adverse winds caused many gliders and paratroopers to be lost. The weather convinced the Italian commanders that an invasion was unlikely, and the Allies therefore secured complete tactical surprise as their forces came ashore under cover of a powerful air armada and heavy gunfire support from the warships patrolling offshore.

The 7th Army was faced by only a single coast defense division manned mainly by Sicilian reservists of low fighting quality

and even lower morale. From the left, the American assault involved Truscott's "Joss" Force (3rd Infantry Division, CCA of the 2nd Armored Division, and a battalion of Rangers that took a beachhead around Licata) and Bradley's II Corps or "Shark" Force (from left to right, "Dime" Force with the 1st Infantry Division and two Ranger battalions that took a beachhead around Gela, "Wolf" Force with the 505th Parachute Infantry Regiment and a battalion of the 504th Parachute Infantry Regiment that took the wrong but still valuable objectives inland of the beaches, and "Cent" Force with the 45th Infantry Division and 753rd Tank Regiment that took two beachheads around Scoglitti and just to the southeast).

Slow Progress at First

Initial development proved difficult because of problems with moving supplies

During the war, the battleship was succeeded by the aircraft carrier as the key to naval power. The battleship still had a significant part to play however. It provided escort for aircraft carriers and heavy gunfire support for ground forces after an amphibious assault. The last U.S. battleships to be built were four of the planned six-strong "Iowa" class, which were the largest battleships ever commissioned by the navy. This photograph shows the first of its class, U.S.S. *Iowa*. She was laid down in New York Navy Yard in June 1940, launched in August 1942, and commissioned in February 1943. Her two catapults each carried a Vought OS2U Kingfisher scout plane. The two cranes were used to recover the aircraft after a waterborne landing.

While landing craft continue their amphibious tasks in the foreground, the problems for the transports and warships lying off the shore of southern Sicily are indicated by the dramatic explosion of a ship hit by a bomb.

from ships to the beaches and the absence of any Allied "air umbrella." This gave the Axis air forces an almost free hand over the beaches, and the Germans took very useful advantage of the fact. On July 10, an Italian division counterattacked the Gela beachhead, but was checked by naval gunfire and infantry. The following day, German armor moved against the same beachhead. It was beaten back by extraordinarily accurate naval gunfire, artillery, infantry, and tanks, but at the cost of the highest American daily casualties of the campaign.

The Allies continued to push forward. On July 13, the Italian commander in Sicily received permission to pull back his mobile forces, including one German and two Italian divisions at the western end of the island, toward the plain of Catania south of Mount Etna. From then on, the Axis defense was one of delay and attrition. The Italians in particular abandoned any hope of driving the Allies back into the sea. Hitler rapidly saw the way events were moving and authorized the movement of additional German forces onto the island.

Between July 12 and 15, the Allies linked up their forces into a single lodgement stretching from a point north of Augusta on the eastern coast to a point south of Agrigento on the southwestern coast. By the 15th, the British were meeting strengthening resistance as their four front-line divisions pushed north toward Catania; at the same time, Patton had been able to group the 2nd Armored and 82nd Airborne Divisions near Gela as the 7th Army reserve.

Evolving Plans

The nature of the Axis defense was now clearer, and on July 15 Alexander issued orders for the next phase of the campaign. The British 8th Army was to advance on Messina, on the northeastern tip of the island, around each side of Mount Etna. The 7th Army was to protect the left flank of the British 8th Army by driving to the north coast of the island and then mopping up any resistance in the western half. On July 17, Patton took Agrigento and Porto Empedocle (which provided additional harbor facilities), but was then faced with the problem of moving his right-hand formation, the 45th Infantry Division, west so that the 1st Canadian Division of the British 8th Army could move around the western side of Mount Etna.

Patton now won Alexander's approval for a drive straight to Palermo. When he received permission, he divided his strength into Bradley's original II Corps (1st and 45th Infantry Divisions) on the right and Major General Geoffrey Keyes's Provisional Corps (2nd Armored, 3rd Infantry, and 82nd Airborne Division) on the left. Keyes's corps had the arduous but straightforward task of clearing western Sicily and taking Palermo, which fell to the 3rd Infantry Division on July 22. II Corps had a harder time and reached the sea between Cefalu and Termini Imerese on July 23.

The British 8th Army was still stalled south and west of Catania, where the

best of the Axis formations were located. On July 20, Alexander modified his plan, instructing the 1st Canadian Division to move closer around the western side of Mount Etna to make room for the 7th Army to change front and advance east along the north coast to Messina with the 1st, 3rd, and 45th Infantry Divisions.

Resistance now stiffened further as more German units arrived on the island, and practical command was assumed by a capable German officer, Colonel General Heinz Hube. Even so, Patton pushed his 1st Infantry Division east along the road from Gangi to Randazzo via Nicosia, and his 45th Infantry Division east along the coast road.

The Germans Take Over the Defense

The Italian forces had begun to leave the island on July 31. A few days later, Hube

This scene is typical of landings in southern Sicily during July 1943. Men and light vehicles were moved from ship to shore in light amphibious craft such as this LCVP (Landing Craft, Vehicle and Personnel) with a ramp bow that could be dropped to allow unloading directly onto the beach. Weightier equipment, such as artillery, tanks, and heavy trucks, was carried in larger vessels such as the medium-sized LCT (Landing Craft, Tank) with a dropping bow ramp or this large LST (Landing Ship, Tank) with a ramp inside outward-opening bow doors. Such ships could deliver their loads directly onto the beach in the right circumstances, but often discharged their vehicles onto a floating pontoon causeway as seen here in front of LST 338.

was authorized to evacuate his forces at his own discretion, for the British 8th Army was threatening the key position at Adrano on the southwestern side of Mount Etna, and the Germans now doubted whether Italy would continue to participate in the war.

German resistance against the U.S. forces was still strengthening, however, and on August 2, the 3rd Infantry Division replaced the 45th Infantry Division for the attack on San Fratello. At much the same time, the 1st Infantry Division was reinforced by a Regimental Combat Team of the 9th Infantry Division for the capture of Troina. The two attacks began on August 3, but made very slow progress. Yet the Germans were now committed to an evacuation of Sicily and slowly fell back. Patton tried unsuccessfully to trap them with three amphibious envelopments and reached Messina on August 17 just after the last of 100,000 or more Germans (including three high-grade divisions) had departed, taking with them 9,800 vehicles and much other equipment.

The Sicilian campaign was over. Axis losses, most of them prisoners, had been 164,000, including 32,000 Germans; the British 8th Army had lost 9,353 men and the 7th Army 7,319.

The Fall of Mussolini: A Factor to Exploit

Shortly after the capture of Palermo, Mussolini was deposed as Italian ruler on July 24. Two days later, the CCS decided that this opportunity should not be lost and ordered Eisenhower to plan and implement an invasion of the Italian mainland.

This change in policy must be seen in perspective. Between May 15 and 25, Roosevelt, Churchill, and the CCS had convened in Washington for the Trident Conference. They reaffirmed the "Germany first" policy, ordered a major intensification of the strategic bombing campaign against Germany and ordered a cross-Channel invasion of Europe through France for May 1, 1944. The

Half-track personnel carriers head inland from the Sicilian beach. Such half-tracks were among the most important American vehicles of the war. They combined the wheeled truck's payload with much of the tracked vehicle's cross-country mobility. Each carried medium and heavy machine guns and provided some armor protection.

The Allied invasion of Sicily prompted the overthrow of the Italian dictator, Benito Mussolini, who was locked away in a remote mountain hotel. Mussolini was later rescued in a daring raid led by Otto Skorzeny, Germany's greatest commando, and installed as head of the puppet Italian regime established by the Germans in northern Italy. As he tried to escape into Germany during the last days of the war, Mussolini was captured by Italian partisans and hanged on April 28, 1945. His body was then hung by its feet in the Piazza Loretto in Milan.

Mark K. Clark
For further references see pages 60, 62, 67, 69, 70

conference also agreed on an increased Allied effort against Japan.

So, an invasion of France in 1944 and a subsequent drive to Germany still had the highest priority. However, the overthrow of Mussolini, and the later opening of secret talks with the incoming Italian government about an Italian capitulation, opened new possibilities. An Allied front in Italy would tie down substantial German forces and therefore improve the chances of a cross-Channel landing in 1944. There were also bonuses. Allied possession of Italian airfields would allow the Allies to carry out strategic bombing of targets in Germany too far south to be attacked effectively from British bases. Italian garrison forces in southern France and the Balkans would probably defect and need replacement by Germans. In addition, the way would be opened for a later conquest of Sardinia and Corsica as

a move toward the invasion of southern France.

Plans for the Allied effort against Japan were enlarged at the Quadrant Conference. Held in Quebec between August 14 and 24, 1943, the conference reached several decisions, including a boost in the war against Japan as long as it did not interfere with the "Germany first" policy, and a hastening of the invasion of Italy.

Plans to Invade Italy

A day after he had received his orders from the CCS, Eisenhower ordered his deputy, Lieutenant General Mark K. Clark, to plan an invasion of southwestern Italy, with landings in the Bay of Salerno just south of Naples. The formation earmarked for this Operation "Avalanche" was the new 5th Army commanded by Clark. The attention of the Germans was to be distracted by a naval demonstration farther north in the Bay of Gaeta, and the whole area was to be softened up by a massive air campaign against airfields and communications.

On September 3, 1943, the Italians signed a secret armistice with the Allies, and on the same day, two British divisions crossed the Strait of Messina into the Calabrian "toe" of Italy. These formations advanced up the north and south sides of the peninsula against negligible opposition; their real task was actually to attract German reinforcements that would then be cut off by the Salerno landing.

Between September 3 and 7, convoys left Oran, Bizerte, Tripoli, and Palermo with the 5th Army. News of the Italian armistice broke late on September 8, and long-term German plans were implemented to disarm the Italian forces and occupy key points in Italy.

Operation "Avalanche"

With the same type of superb naval gunfire support that had been available for "Husky," together with much improved air cover, the 5th Army began to land in the Bay of Salerno. The half of the operation north of the Sele River

51

THE CAMPAIGN IN ITALY

Map labels:

AUSTRIA
SWITZERLAND
HUNGARY
Line reached by Allied forces in Western Europe, 7 May, 1945
Line reached by Russian Forces 7 May, 1945
Brenner Pass
Danube
The Alps
Adige
Drava
TRENTO
UDINE
COMO
VERONA
PADUA
TRIESTE
Sava
TURIN
MILAN
PIACENZA
VENICE
Po
FRANCE
GENOA
BOLOGNA
RAVENNA 25 Sept. 1944
23 Apr
15 Jan 8-Apr. 1945
Line reached by Yugoslav Partisans 7 May, 1945
YUGOSLAVIA
Gothic Line
RIMINI
Arno
FLORENCE
SAN MARINO
PESARO 26 Aug. 1944
LEGHORN
CECINA
AREZZO
ANCONA
POGGISONSI
PEBUGIA
ELBA
9 June
17 June
Corsica
Evacuated by German Forces, 18 Sept-3 Oct, 1943
ORVIETO
TERNI
River Tiber
PESCARA
ADRIATIC SEA
Gustav Line
8 Oct. 1943
26 Sept
Allies enter Rome 4 June, 1944
ROME 5 June
19 Feb
ANZIO
TERRACINA
CASSINO
FOGGIA
25 Sept
14 Sept
BARI
Sardinia
Evacuated by German Forces 18 Sept, 1943
Op "Shingle" 22 Jan, 1944
GAETA
NAPLES
SALERNO
BRINDISI
TARANTO
CAGLIARI
TYRRHENIAN SEA
AULETTA
Op "Avalanche" 9 Sept, 1943
14 Sept
Op "Slapstick" 9 Sept, 1943
CORIGLIANO CALABRO
14 Sept
3 Sept, 1943
Italy surrenders
9 Sept
Op "Baytown" 3 Sept, 1943
MESSINA
REGGIO
TRAPANI
PALERMO
LUNA
17 Aug
ALGERIA
Sicily
CATANIA
23 July
SYRACUSE
TUNISIA
LICATA
ENNA
AVOLA
PANTELLERIA 11 June
Op "Husky" 10 June, 1943
LINOSA
MALTA (Br)

FRONT LINE AT DATE SHOWN
US FIFTH ARMY
BRITISH EIGHTH ARMY

MILES 0 — 200
KILOMETERS 0 — 300

The Italian campaign, which lasted from July 1943 to May 1945, was very hard fought. U.S. forces were mainly deployed west of the Apennine mountain range.

was entrusted to the British X Corps, and the half south of the river mouth to Major General Ernest J. Dawley's VI Corps, whose initial landing formation was Major General Fred L. Walker's reinforced 36th Infantry Division. The core of the German defense was the 16th Panzer Division, the most forward element of Colonel General Heinrich-Gottfried von Vietinghoff-Scheel's German 10th Army, well placed behind good defenses.

By nightfall, the Allies had secured only four small and unconnected beachheads, around Paestum in the sector of VI Corps. Kesselring had anticipated that the Gulf of Salerno was one of the most likely invasion spots and immediately began to move reinforcements into the area. The Salerno beachhead battle lasted from September 10 to 14, when the Germans had most of six divisions in the area, together with powerful artillery on the commanding heights with an almost perfect view over the beachheads.

The Americans and British were able to drive their way a little more inland, but while the three northern beachheads were able to link up, it proved impossible to extend this consolidation south across the gap between Battipaglia and the Sele

River to include the beachhead of the 36th Infantry Division, which was reinforced from September 10 by elements of Major General Troy H. Middleton's 45th Infantry Division.

On September 12, the Germans launched a powerful offensive into the Allied center and nearly succeeded in splitting the 5th Army before American artillery and naval gunfire halted them just short of the beach the following day. The shortage of Allied shipping made seaborne reinforcement impossible, but the situation in the beachhead was so desperate that, during the night of September 12, two battalions of the 82nd Airborne Division were parachuted into the southern half of the perimeter.

Despite their exhaustion, the Germans continued during September 14 with a series of probing attacks, but Allied naval gunfire and tactical aircraft played a decisive part in checking any further German progress. By the following day, Allied reinforcements were pouring into the beachhead to stabilize the position, and the day after that, the leading elements of the British 8th Army arrived from Calabria to establish contact with the right-hand units of VI Corps.

On September 9, a British division had made an extemporized landing at Taranto on the Italian "heel," and this important port became the main base for the British 8th Army during its advance up the eastern side of Italy.

The Germans Concede a Partial Defeat

Between September 16 and 18, the Germans disengaged from Salerno and pulled back to the north after suffering about 8,000 casualties. The Allied losses had been about 15,000 men.

The operational advantage now lay with the Allies, who consolidated their position in southern Italy between September 18 and October 8. Operating on the western side of the Apennine Mountains which form Italy's backbone, the 5th Army took Naples on October 2 and continued north until the swollen Volturno River halted them six days later. On the other side of the mountains, the

British 8th Army pressed as far north as Termoli on the coast of the Adriatic Sea by the same date.

By this time, the Allies had achieved the initial objectives of their Italian campaign: Italy had surrendered, the Germans had left Sardinia and Corsica, the complex of airfields around Foggia was now in Allied hands for raids into southern and central Europe, and Germany had been forced to rush troops into Italy and the Balkans. Purely military logic dictated that the Allies could now have gone onto the defensive, pinning the German forces by their very presence, or forcing the Germans to accept the higher losses involved in attacking the Allies and trying to drive them back into the sea.

Another point of view, and the one that prevailed, urged further Allied advance. The arguments in favor of this move were the vulnerability of Rome, whose capture would be a political and morale coup for the Allies, the availability of many more airfields around Rome, and the informa-

Lieutenant General Mark W. Clark made his name as commander of the 5th Army in the Italian campaign. He later succeeded a British officer as commander-in-chief of Allied forces in Italy.

The Germans reacted to the Allied landing at Salerno in September 1943 with a major air effort. The Allied ships responded to attacks with concentrated antiaircraft fire, which at night was made visible by the paths of tracer rounds.

tion, already known to the Allies, that the Germans had made initial preparations to fall back into northern Italy and might therefore need only a nudge to implement this plan.

It soon became clear, however, that the Germans were prepared to fight in southern Italy, and the Allied commanders feared that unless they attacked, the strategic initiative would be seized by the Germans.

The terrain certainly favored the German plans, for the 100 or more miles between the Volturno River and Rome lying across the Allied line of advance were a jumble of mountains cut by rivers and ravines. It was ideal country for using delaying tactics, which was just what the Germans planned against Allied forces untrained and ill-equipped for mountain warfare in the dismal wetness of fall and bitter cold of winter. The obvious Allied tactic in this situation would be a series of amphibious operations allowing the

Allied forces to bypass German defensive positions, but the Germans knew that the Allied shortage of amphibious warfare ships made this move improbable.

The Drive to the "Gustav" Line

To buy time for his engineers to complete the defensive positions which he expected his troops to hold through the winter, Kesselring ordered the German 10th Army to hold its current positions until at least October 15. The formation facing the 5th Army west of the Apennines was XIV Panzer Corps with four high-quality divisions. After careful reconnaissance, the 5th Army attacked on October 12, with the British X Corps on the left and Major General John P. Lucas's VI Corps on the right. Each corps deployed three divisions in the front line.

The fighting was very bitter, but on October 13, five of the six divisions won a

Left: American M4 Sherman medium tanks come ashore at Salerno. The presence of such tanks in the landing area was vital to the defeat of the Germans' intense effort to eliminate the four small initial Allied beachheads before they could be linked up.

Below: American troops wait at the docks in Palermo, in northwestern Sicily, before embarking to reinforce the Salerno operation.

Many items of German equipment were of very high quality. When the Allied forces lacked adequate weapons of their own, they often used captured equipment. Seen here in the hands of an American antiaircraft detachment protecting Rome from the possibility of German air attack in July 1944 is a Flakvierling antiaircraft gun. This hand-operated equipment mounted four 20-mm cannon that could put up a veritable wall of short-range fire.

bridgehead across the Volturno River. The three American bridgeheads were soon consolidated into a single lodgement stretching as far down the river as Capua. German artillery fire prevented the Allied engineers from bridging the river until October 14 and 15, and only then did the Germans slowly pull back as the Allied divisions edged forward. The British 8th Army had been forced to regroup before resuming the offensive, which it did on October 22 before forcing a crossing of the Trigno River.

The German 10th Army's defense of the Volturno and Trigno river crossings had bought Kesselring the time he needed for the completion of the main winter position, the so-called "Gustav" Line running from the coast of the Tyrrhenian Sea up the Garigliano River, across the Apennines, and then down the Sangro River to the Adriatic Sea. The 5th Army fought its way slowly toward this major position. In the process, it reached an intermediate position known as the "Barbara" Line in the western sector and the "Bernhard" Line in the eastern sector. As the Allies forced their way toward the "Gustav" Line, they were faced by stiffening German resistance, extensive demolitions, mines, and booby traps. Deteriorating weather turned roads into mud slides and washed away the temporary bridges they had put up to replace

U.S. and British field ambulances deliver casualties to a British hospital ship docked in the harbor of Naples. In the background is a burned out liner, the *Lombardia*.

the permanent structures demolished by the Germans. In these circumstances, it is hardly surprising that the soldiers of the 5th and British 8th Armies were completely exhausted when the 15th Army Group called a halt to the offensive on November 13, with its forces closed up against the intermediate position known to the Allies as the "Winter" Line.

Modified Plans

With the exception of a single narrow-gauge railroad down the east coast, all railborne supplies for the German 10th Army had to pass through the area around Rome. This created a strategic situation which Alexander thought ripe for a crushing German defeat after an amphibious landing near Rome had cut the German lines of communication and isolated the German 10th Army south of the city. On November 8, therefore, Alexander issued orders for a three-phase offensive. In the first phase, the British 8th Army would advance northwest to

Pescara and then wheel inland along the good road toward Avezzano. In the second phase, the 5th Army would attack up the valleys of the Liri and Sacco Rivers toward Frosinone. In the third phase, one corps would undertake an amphibious assault south of Rome and then sweep inland to take the Alban Hills, completing the trap in which the German forces could then be destroyed.

The plan was difficult to implement, for seven veteran divisions were being shipped out to the United Kingdom for the planned cross-Channel operation, while the French divisions to replace them were still being trained in North Africa. As usual, both conventional and amphibious shipping was in short supply, a situation made worse by the arrival of the Allies' first heavy bomber units with their consequent demand for fuel and munitions. Alexander made strong representations that amphibious ships in the Mediterranean should remain there, but received grudging permission from the CCS to retain them only until January 15, 1944, when they would sail for the United Kingdom.

Above: The Germans skillfully sowed defensive minefields that either blocked Allied advances or channeled them into targeted killing zones where the artillery could do terrible damage. The Allies responded with a number of ingenious mine-clearing derivatives of standard tanks. This is a Mine Exploder M1, also known as an Aunt Jemima, which was produced in small numbers during 1943. The vehicle was the M4 Sherman medium tank. It used a roller chain arrangement to drive the 30-ton exploder, which was made up of twin roller units, each containing five 10-foot diameter steel disks. These disks had the weight and solidity to detonate mines without suffering significant damage themselves.

Right: The army's most important tank of World War II was the Medium Tank M4. The British called the tank "Sherman," and this name soon became universal. The Sherman was produced by several manufacturers in a series of variants. The various models differed most radically in their engines, for there were not enough 400-horsepower Continental R-975 air-cooled radial engines to satisfy demand. In its original form, the M4 had a cast hull, and a cast turret, mounting a 75-mm gun. The Sherman was standardized in October 1941, and vast numbers were produced. The type illustrated in this cutaway view is an M4A4, which was standardized in February 1942. It was basically the same as the original M4 in everything but its engine, a 425-horsepower Chrysler water-cooled unit. It was produced by combining five car engine cylinder banks onto a single crankcase and crankshaft. The installation meant that the hull had to be lengthened by 6 inches. The M4A4 weighed 34·2 tons and was manned by a crew of five. It had a maximum speed of 25 miles an hour on roads, averaging 15 miles an hour cross-country, and a range of 120 and about 80 miles respectively. The hull and turret fronts were 2 and 2.5 inches thick, and the armament included one 75-mm gun with 97 rounds, two 0·3-inch machine guns with 6,750 rounds (one in the bow and the other aligned with the main armament), and one 0·5-inch machine gun with 300 rounds on the turret roof.

American infantry soldiers assemble in combat teams before embarking in their amphibious assault vessels. The loading of units and formations with their equipment in the right order became one of the most important planning considerations of World War II. It meant that combat troops arrived on the assault beach with the right weapons and other equipment; and that supplies and other equipment were readily available when they were needed.

This placed a limit on the time available for the 15th Army Group's offensive, which faced a truly formidable task against skilled and determined opponents. The Germans were in excellently sited positions that took every advantage of the mountainous terrain and could be approached only along routes that had been mined and registered by the Germans' artillery.

The "Gustav" Line Campaign

The British 8th Army moved off under cover of all available Allied air power on November 20 and almost immediately secured a number of small bridgeheads across the Sangro River. Then torrential rain intervened, and further operations had to be postponed until November 27. By December 2, the entire British 8th Army was across the Sangro River and pushing on toward Pescara against wors-

ening weather and strengthening German resistance. It became increasingly difficult to supply the front-line troops. Tanks bogged down in the universal mud, and lack of reserves meant that localized successes could not be exploited adequately. The result was ever-slowing progress and an ever-increasing casualty rate. The British 8th Army had no option but to call off its offensive on January 15, 1944. It was still short of Pescara but had actually broken through the "Gustav" Line defenses at the eastern end.

The story was much the same for the 5th Army, which began its offensive on December 1, 1943. From left to right, Clark committed the British X Corps, Keyes's II Corps, and Lucas's VI Corps (which was relieved from the beginning of January by the French Expeditionary Corps). The fighting was bitter and the weather appalling, and before the offensive was called off on January 15, 1944, the 5th Army had fought its way forward

Known formally as the Gun M1A1 on Carriage M1, but more commonly as the "Long Tom," this weapon was the army's most important piece of heavy artillery in World War II. It had been standardized in 1938 and was already in production when the United States entered war. The "Long Tom" served in most theaters, operated by 14-man crews. The complete equipment weighed 30,600 pounds on the move behind its 6 x 6-foot tractor and dropped to 27,775 pounds in firing position. It fired a 127-pound projectile to a maximum range of 25,700 yards. The rate of fire was one round per minute.

to the "Gustav" Line, but had not managed to breach it anywhere.

Under the circumstances, it was inevitable that the amphibious third phase of the operation had to be postponed. December 1943 also saw a major Allied reorganization of its command in the Mediterranean. Eisenhower moved to the United Kingdom to assume overall command of the Allied forces preparing for the cross-Channel invasion and was replaced by a British officer. General Sir Bernard Montgomery also returned to the United Kingdom to take over field command of the invasion forces and was replaced as British 8th Army commander by General Sir Oliver Leese. In the same month, the Germans created their Army Group "C" under Kesselring to hold Italy.

The fighting to break through the "Winter" Line and to close up on the defenses of the "Gustav" Line itself was fierce. It became perfectly plain that any offensive to penetrate this dominating position, the core of the German defenses south of Rome, would be slow and immensely heavy in casualties.

Dire Days at Cassino

The key point of the "Gustav" Line was Cassino, a solidly built town lying in the junction of the Rápido and Liri Rivers on the southeastern edge of Mount Cairo. This was the focal point of the 15th Army Group's revised offensive scheme. The British X Corps was to make a secondary attack across the lower reaches of the Garigliano River to suck in the German reserves. This would ease the task of II Corps in attacking up the Liri River valley toward Frosinone and of the French Expeditionary Corps in working their way into the mountains north of Cassino. When these concerted operations were well underway, VI Corps would land at Anzio in an amphibious assault to take the Alban Hills. The resulting threat to the German 10th Army's line of communications would hopefully cause it to fall back from the "Gustav" Line, probably to points north of Rome.

While the 5th Army undertook this complex operation, the British 8th Army would continue its effort to reach Pes-

Bernard Montgomery
For further references see pages
72, 73, 84, 87, 89, 92, 95, 102, 103, 104, 105, 109, 111, 115, 120

Operation "Shingle"

With the German reserves sucked into the fighting along the Rapido River, Alexander felt the time was ripe for Operation "Shingle," the amphibious assault at Anzio. The formation allocated for the task was VI Corps, which sailed from Naples on January 21. The unit achieved a virtually unopposed landing of 50,000 men and 5,200 vehicles the following day with elements of one British division, supported by commandos, and Truscott's 3rd Infantry Division, supported by Rangers and a battalion of the 509th Parachute Infantry Regiment. Lucas decided not to gamble on a fast move into the Alban Hills, which might have left Rome open as a target, but instead consolidated thoroughly in his beachhead. Kesselring had anticipated such a move, and from January 23, he stripped quiet sectors of the "Gustav" Line to combine with formations from northern Italy to create Colonel General Eberhard von Mackensen's German 14th Army.

Lucas made his first effort to drive inland on January 30, but was pinned down in the beachhead by powerful armored, mechanized, and infantry forces. With VI Corps trapped, the Germans bided their time until bad weather on February 15 grounded Allied aircraft and made naval gunfire support difficult. They then unleashed a major attack that made good progress through February 16 and 17. The Allied position was extremely precarious on February 18, but the German commander did not commit his whole reserve at this decisive point. On February 19, VI Corps counterattacked and stabilized its position. The Germans launched a number of smaller attacks up to February 29, but none of them seriously threatened VI Corps, in which Truscott replaced Lucas as commander on February 23.

From the beginning of March 1944, the Germans fortified their positions containing VI Corps, and the battle for the Anzio beachhead became a siege.

At Cassino, the position was even more difficult and costly. In the first week of February 1944, Ryder's 34th Infantry Division tried to envelop Cassino from the

By 1944, the Douglas SBD Dauntless was outdated as a dive-bomber operating from the navy's fleet carriers for the first-line role against enemy warships. It still had a useful part to play in operations against submarines, however, and operated from escort carriers and land bases in these operations.

cara, despite being weakened by the transfer of units to strengthen the 5th Army.

The British X Corps kicked off the offensive on January 17, 1944, and soon secured a useful bridgehead across the Garigliano River. By January 20, the growing size and threat of this bridgehead had attracted all available German reserves. Farther up the river, the 36th Infantry Division of II Corps attempted a similar feat, but was repulsed with heavy losses between January 17 and 19. Still more to the north, the French Expeditionary Corps made progress, though only at considerable cost, in its effort to nibble into the German positions in the mountains. Clark saw the French progress as offering some promise and ordered a Franco-American effort in this sector with the object of enveloping Cassino from the north as the French shifted their axis from northwest and west to southwest in the direction of Piedimonte.

north, but was forced to a halt on February 12. The newly created New Zealand Corps then replaced II Corps and attacked between February 15 and 18 with enormous courage, but with an equal lack of success. A third assault was ordered as a limited offensive to gain the small bridgehead across the Rapido River, which was needed as the launch point for a planned drive up the valley of the Liri River. Cassino was pounded for hours by bombers and massed artillery before the ground offensive was sent in. The attackers soon discovered that the pounding had destroyed the town and turned it into an almost impenetrable maze of collapsed masonry that favored the German 1st Parachute Division far more than the attackers. By March 23, the Germans had fought the Allies to a complete standstill on the edge of Cassino.

Alexander now shifted the boundary between the 5th Army and the British 8th Army to the south so that fresher forces

(the British XIII Corps and the Polish Corps) could be brought to bear on Cassino. He also increased the strength in the Anzio beachhead to seven divisions (five American, including one armored, and two British). This allowed the offensive to be resumed. The main task was given to the British 8th Army, which was to push up the valley of the Liri and Sacco Rivers toward Valmontone. The 5th Army was to break out of its Garigliano River bridgehead and advance along the coast. There, it was to link up with VI Corps after the latter had smashed out of its beachhead toward Valmontone later in the offensive, with the task of trapping the German forces falling back before the British 8th Army.

Success at Cassino

The offensive started on May 11 and achieved complete tactical surprise. The

Men of the Special Service Force move up to the front in their Light Cargo Carrier T24. These men, all volunteers, were the first to cross the Rapido River with medical supplies and food for the assault infantry in the bitter fighting between February and May 1944.

Germans soon recovered, and it was May 18 before Cassino finally fell. Nearer the coast, the French Expeditionary Corps and the two American divisions of II Corps made good progress. On May 25, they linked up with the leading elements of II Corps. It appeared that the German 10th Army was virtually in the bag, but at this point Clark shifted the axis of the 5th Army advance from north to northwest, and the 5th Army entered Rome on June 4. The rearguards of the German 10th Army held back the Americans at Valmontone and Velletri, and the bulk of the army escaped.

Kesselring's problem was now twofold. First, he had to pull back the German 10th and 14th Armies (the latter now commanded by General Joachim Lemelsen) to the major defenses of the "Gothic" Line. At the same time, he had to implement the German withdrawal in a manner that would hold back the Allied ad-

vance. Any delay would buy time needed for the completion of the "Gothic" Line positions, which ran from the Tyrrhenian Sea at a point south of La Spezia to the Adriatic Sea near Pesaro. Within this twin strategic task, Kesselring also had to achieve the withdrawal under conditions of total Allied air superiority.

Speedy Advance

Initially, the Allies swept forward without any hindrance except the need to lift German mines and repair the destruction caused by German demolition teams. All was apparently set fair for a major Allied success in Italy, and Alexander was confident that his strong, well-supplied forces would be able to break through the incomplete "Gothic" Line defenses and advance into the valley of the Po River during August 1944.

A 105 mm howitzer is brought ashore near Naples. Chicken wire was laid onto the beach to avoid vehicles sinking in the sand.

Alexander felt that two options would then be open to his armies: either an advance westward into southern France, or eastward toward Venice and southern Austria. The British preferred the latter and suggested that the planned Allied invasion of southern France be cancelled so that strong forces would be available in Italy for the destruction of Army Group ''C'' and a drive into southern Austria. The Americans found it difficult even to consider such a move, for they remained totally convinced that the major port of Marseille in southern France had to be captured if the main Allied campaign against Germany through France were to succeed.

The invasion of southern France had also been approved at the Eureka Conference between Roosevelt, Churchill, and Soviet leader Joseph Stalin, which met in Tehran, Persia, between November 28 and 30, 1943. Roosevelt now felt that the invasion of southern France could not be cancelled without Stalin's permission. Another factor that had to be considered was the growing desire of the French forces in Italy to fight for the liberation of their homeland.

Churchill finally agreed with Roosevelt, and the 5th Army lost seven divisions, including all the formations of the French Expeditionary Corps in Italy. The loss of these first-line formations was bad enough in itself, but their withdrawal toward southern Italian ports, involving movement in the direction opposite to the supplies and equipment flowing north, completely destroyed Alexander's scheduling. The move also deprived the Allied forces in Italy of their only mountain troops, and also one bomber group and 23 fighter squadrons. The only replacements offered were two infantry divisions, one American and the other Brazilian, due to arrive in September and

German soldiers surrender to an American infantry/armor team at Cisterna on May 25, 1944. On this day, American forces advancing from the Rapido River front linked up with men of VI Corps after their breakout from the Anzio lodgement.

Joseph Stalin
For further references
see pages
72, *122*

The driver of a Sherman tank of the 1st Armored Division's 1st Tank Battalion in Italy during August 1944. Beside the driver is the open hatch of his position, complete with the periscope which allowed him to operate in the "battened down" condition.

October respectively. Taking all these factors into account, the CCS ordered Alexander to advance to the line between Verona and Venice via Padua.

On the other side of the front, Kesselring had received eight more divisions, which allowed him to create a holding line across Italy soutrh of Lake Trasimeno by June 17. Aided by minefields and demolitions, and the sacrifice of second-rate units, the Germans now began to buy the time they needed to complete the "Gothic" Line. Thus it was only on August 4 that the two Allied armies finally began to reach the outer positions of this formidable defensive position between Pisa and Ribbiena via Florence. In the previous 64 days, the Allies had advanced an average of 270 miles.

Stalled in Front of the "Gothic" Line

Alexander had planned to use his Moroccan mountain troops to break past the Futa Pass and descend on Bologna without a pause. The removal of these units meant that another plan was needed, and on August 4, the Allied armies paused for three weeks. In this time, the balance of the Allied forces across Italy altered radically. The main weight of the British 8th Army was shifted east toward the Adriatic coast, and the 5th Army was reinforced with the British XIII Corps. The plan was for the British 8th Army to smash through the Germans' eastern defense, which was thought to be comparatively

weak, and advance on Bologna via Rimini and Ravenna. Meanwhile, the 5th Army's preparations would make the Germans believe that the main Allied attack was to be launched from Florence toward Bologna. Only when the Germans had been disabused of this idea by the British 8th Army's advance, and responded by moving formations east, would the 5th Army commit its II and British XIII Corps toward Bologna and Ferrara.

The Allied plan was implemented from August 25 and initially worked like clockwork as first the British 8th Army and then the 5th Army drove through the "Gothic" Line defenses. Then, improvised defenses of the typically dogged German type began to break the momentum of the Allied advance. This slowing down

process was completed by the advent of appalling weather that slowed the arrival of supplies and made movement all but impossible. Clark committed his last reserves on October 1 in an effort to reach Bologna, but this desperate effort was halted just nine miles short of its objective on October 20.

A Lull in Italy

The two Allied armies were exhausted, and replacements had failed to keep pace with casualties. Ammunition was also in short supply. Early in December, Alexander launched a limited offensive to prevent the Germans from moving formations from Italy, and though the British

DUKW amphibious trucks ferry supplies across the beach during the hectic opening days of Operation "Shingle," the landing of VI Corps at Anzio during January 1944.

67

Above: A 105-mm howitzer under camouflage netting pounds German positions in the "Gothic Line" toward its western end near Lucca.

Left: Engineers of the 92nd (Negro) Division sweep a beach for German mines. In this operation, 78 mines were found in one section just 50 feet square.

An ordnance sergeant of the U.S. Army gives food to a pair of Italian children.

8th Army made some progress, the 5th Army was effectively trapped in the mountains by the weather. Late in the month, a German counteroffensive down the valley of the Serchio River toward Pisa made some progress, but was then checked. On January 15, 1945, a lull settled over the Italian front, which was destined to last three months as the Allies digested the unpalatable fact that Italian victory had escaped them in 1944. There were considerable command changes on both sides of the front. On the German side, Kesselring was recalled to help in the defense of the German fatherland and was replaced by one of his capable army commanders, von Vietinghoff-Scheel, as commander of what was now Army Group "Southwest." On the Allied side, Alexander was promoted to Mediterranean command and replaced at the head of the 15th Army Group by Clark, whose position as commander of the 5th Army was assumed by Lieutenant General Truscott.

Despite the fact that the Soviets were within 40 miles of Berlin on April 1, 1945, Germany was determined not to surrender. In Italy, the men of Army Group "Southwest" prepared new defensive positions along the lines of the Po and Adige Rivers after Hitler refused to allow von Vietinghoff-Scheel to plan and implement a secret withdrawal over the Po River, the only sensible move, given the fact that the Germans lacked both the strength to check an Allied offensive and the mobility to fall back in good order after failing to check such an offensive.

The three-month lull allowed the Allied armies to rest, reorganize, and re-equip. Thus refreshed, they were a formidable

Half-tracks of the 1st
Armored Division in
northern Italy.

foe who knew that only a few miles of mountains separated them from the valley of the Po River.

Alexander and Clark planned their 1945 offensive with great care with the hope of trapping and defeating the German forces on the southern side of the Po River. The British 8th Army was to move first to try to clear the Adriatic coast before moving on Ferrara. Five days later, the 5th Army would attack, with the task of capturing Bologna and approaching Bondeno near Ferrara. There, it would link up with the British 8th Army to cross the Po River and take Verona, so cutting

the Germans' line of retreat toward western Austria.

The End in Italy

The British got underway on April 9, and the Americans followed on April 14. There was initially some severe fighting as the Germans resisted with their customary determination, but as their ammunition began to run low, Allied aircraft roamed the sky unopposed. As they swooped to destroy anything German that moved, the Germans finally began to break and stream back toward the Po River, abandoning all their heavy weapons and equipment as they went. The Allies poured across the Po in pursuit, and the last effective German resistance crumbled on April 25. The Allied armies fanned out in pursuit, making enormous and virtually unopposed advances until, on April 29, von Vietinghoff-Scheel agreed to an unconditional surrender that became effective at midday on May 2.

Planning the Cross-Channel Invasion

While the campaign that produced this first theater capitulation by German forces was unfolding, American forces had also become involved as the major partner in the Allied invasion of France. American planners had long campaigned for this move, because they believed that a concentration of mass hurled directly at the principal enemy was the only way to win.

In June 1942, the United States created its European Theater of Operations, and at General Marshall's suggestion, command was entrusted to Major General Eisenhower. Allied plans for an invasion of France in 1943 had been delayed for a number of reasons. The decision to begin proper planning for the invasion was taken at the Casablanca Conference in January 1943, while at the Eureka

With admirable military logic, the Germans demolished all river bridges as they retreated. Allied engineers therefore faced a huge task creating temporary bridges that would allow supplies to reach front-line forces. This is a 210-foot trestle bridge over the Serchio River.

This Apennine forest was shattered by American artillery fire as the Allies battered their way through the defenses of the ''Gothic Line.''

Conference in December 1943, Roosevelt and Churchill informed Stalin that the invasion would be launched late in May or early in June, 1944. In February 1944, the planning group was absorbed into Eisenhower's Supreme Headquarters, Allied Expeditionary Force, and in the next three months, SHAEF finalized the plan for Operation ''Overlord.''

Inter-Allied Command Structure

Under Eisenhower's overall command with a British second in command (Air Chief Marshal Sir Arthur Tedder) and an American chief of staff (Lieutenant General Walter Bedell Smith), the Allied land, sea, and air commanders for the invasion were all British. There was considerable pressure for the American forces involved in the invasion to come under American field command, but Eisenhower decided that Montgomery should command during the invasion itself, and that only later, after consolidation, would separate American and British army groups be established.

General Dwight D. Eisenhower, commanding the Supreme Headquarters, Allied Expeditionary Forces, emphasizes a final point to U.S. paratroops on June 5, 1944, the eve of D-Day for the invasion of Normandy. Together with the men of the British 6th Airborne Division, these American paratroopers and their gliderborne companions of the 82nd and 101st Airborne Divisions spearheaded the Allied effort.

The original plan called for an initial landing by one airborne and three ground divisions, a total considered too small by Eisenhower and Montgomery. The definitive plan called for an initial assault by three airborne and five ground divisions in an area that had to be widened from the one originally conceived.

Pas-de-Calais or Normandy?

A key consideration in fixing the point for the invasion was that it had to lie within range of fighters operating from southern England. It was at first planned that the landings would be made in the Pas-de-Calais region, which offered adequate beaches as well as a short sea crossing from the United Kingdom. However, the fact that the Germans had stationed particularly powerful forces in this region suggested that the location was too obvious. It was finally decided to land in Normandy, considerably farther west.

This meant a longer crossing, but the chosen invasion points were less well protected and further from reinforcement.

The date selected as D-Day for "Overlord" was June 5, 1944, but the invasion had to be postponed at the last minute because of bad weather. The plan called for an assault by Montgomery's 21st Army Group over five beaches. On the left was the British 2nd Army, which was to land three corps on three beaches between Ouistreham in the east and Port-en-Bessin in the west. On the right was Lieutenant General Bradley's 1st Army, which was to land Major General Leonard T. Gerow's V Corps over "Omaha" Beach between Sainte Honorine and Pointe de la Percee, and Major General J. Lawton Collins's VII Corps over "Utah" Beach between Pouppeville and Les Dunes de Varreville.

This left a gap of about ten miles between the two American beaches, and to provide VII Corps with flank protection from Cherbourg, it was decided to drop

Opposite: Last-minute checks for the men of an American mechanized unit before they and their half-tracks board their landing craft for the invasion of Normandy.

Right: American infantry rehearse an assault landing in preparation for Operation "Overlord," the assault on Normandy.

Below: The preparations for Operation "Overlord" were often undertaken in idyllic settings. In this scene, LCT 495 is passing H.M.S. *Loch Park*, one of hundreds of fishing vessels requisitioned by the British for use as minesweepers.

Right: This scene was typical of many ports in southern England before the start of Operation "Overlord." LCTs are waiting here to load their cargo of Jeeps.

Opposite: Final preparations before the invasion of Normandy in June 1944, as crew and troops board ship at a British coast resort.

Above: American infantry on board British LCAs (Landing Craft, Assault) in a small harbor on the British south coast before moving out for the invasion of Normandy.

Major General Matthew B. Ridgway's 82nd Airborne Division and Major General Maxwell D. Taylor's 101st Airborne Division slightly inland from the assault beach. In addition to holding the potentially vulnerable right flank that might be attacked by forces from the powerful German garrison in Cherbourg, the airborne divisions were intended to seize the area into which VII Corps could expand rapidly.

The Allied plan called for the five initial but separate beachheads to be consolidated into what was in essence a single unit by nightfall, though the combined estuary of the Vire, Taute, and Douve Rivers northeast of Carentan would still divide VII Corps from the rest of the Allied position.

Rapid Build Up

"Overlord" demanded the rapid arrival of forces to bolster and develop the beachhead. "Omaha" Beach was to be invaded by Major General Clarence R. Huebner's 1st Infantry Division, which was to be followed by Major General Charles H. Gerhardt's 29th Infantry Division, and then between June 7 and 8, and June 10 and 13 respectively, by Major General Walter M. Robertson's 2nd Infantry Division and the 2nd Armored Division. "Utah" Beach was to be invaded by Major General Raymond O. Barton's 4th Infantry Division, which was to be followed between June 6 and 9, and June 10 and 13 respectively, by Brigadier General Jay W. MacKelvie's 90th Infantry

The nature of the Allied strategic bombing campaign was transformed by the Republic P-47 Thunderbolt Lockheed P-38 Lightning, and North American P-51 Mustang as long-range fighter escorts for the American daylight bombers.

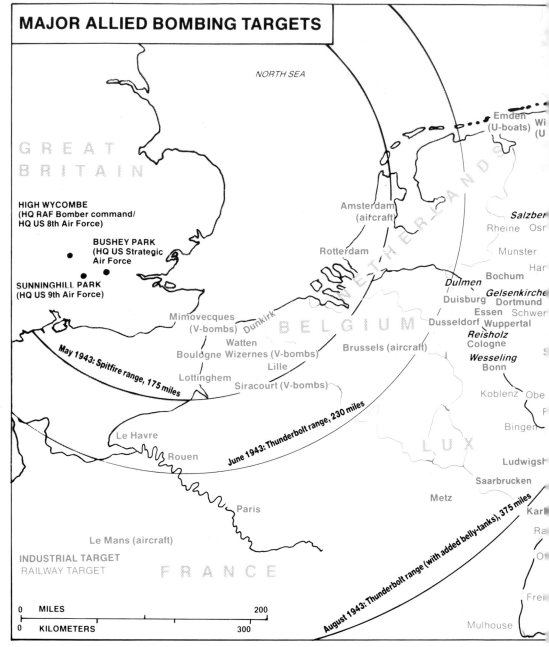

MAJOR ALLIED BOMBING TARGETS

NORTH SEA

GREAT BRITAIN

HIGH WYCOMBE
(HQ RAF Bomber command/
HQ US 8th Air Force)

BUSHEY PARK
(HQ US Strategic
Air Force)

SUNNINGHILL PARK
(HQ US 9th Air Force)

Emden
(U-boats)   Wi
(U

Amsterdam
(aircraft)   Salzber
Rheine   Osr

Rotterdam   Munster

Bochum

Dulmen   Har

Duisburg   Gelsenkirche
Dortmund
Essen   Schwer
Dusseldorf Wuppertal

Reisholz
Cologne

Wesseling
Bonn

Mimovecques
(V-bombs)   Dunkirk
Watten
Bouldgne Wizernes (V-bombs)
Lottinghem
Siracourt (V-bombs)

Brussels (aircraft)

Lille

May 1943: Spitfire range, 175 miles

Le Havre
Rouen

June 1943: Thunderbolt range, 230 miles

Koblenz   Obe

Binger

Ludwigsh

Saarbrucken

Metz

Paris

Le Mans (aircraft)

INDUSTRIAL TARGET
RAILWAY TARGET

FRANCE

August 1943: Thunderbolt range (with added belly-tanks), 375 miles

Kar
Ra
O
Frei

Mulhouse

| 0 | MILES | 200 |
| 0 | KILOMETERS | 300 |

Division and the 9th Infantry Division. As the initial lodgement was expanded, additional forces, including VIII and XIX Corps, would arrive to turn the 1st Army into a truly formidable fighting formation.

Some 4,000 ships and landing craft carried 176,000 men and vast quantities of materiel for the invasion, and this force was escorted by 600 Allied warships. Months of pre-invasion air attacks on the whole area were followed in the last hours before the landings by a deluge of bombs (including 10,000 tons dropped by 3,467 heavy bombers that mustered 1,083 American machines in their number) and the lighter weapons of 7,054 twin-engined bombers and single-engined fighter bombers that ripped though the area.

Operation "Overlord"

The landings were ably covered by naval gunfire and took the Germans completely by surprise. By nightfall, the five assault divisions were ashore, and all but the 1st Infantry Division had established

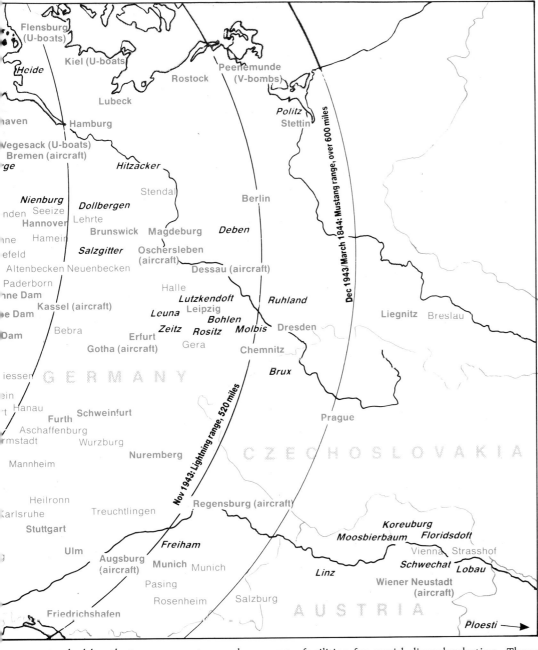

Flensburg
(U-boats)

Kiel (U-boats)

Heide

Rostock

Peenemunde
(V-bombs)

Lubeck

Politz

haven

Hamburg

Stettin

Vegesack (U-boats)
Bremen (aircraft)

rge

Hitzacker

Stendal

Berlin

Nienburg

Seeize

Dollbergen

nden

Lehrte

Deben

Hannover

Brunswick

Magdeburg

ne

Hamein

Salzgitter

Oschersleben
(aircraft)

efeld

Altenbecken

Neuenbecken

Dessau (aircraft)

Paderborn

Halle

nne Dam

Lutzkendoft

Kassel (aircraft)

Leuna

Leipzig

Ruhland

Liegnitz

Breslau

e Dam

Bohlen

Dam

Bebra

Zeitz

Rositz

Molbis

Dresden

Erfurt

Gotha (aircraft)

Gera

Chemnitz

iessen

G E R M A N Y

Brux

ein

Hanau

Schweinfurt

t

Furth

Prague

Aschaffenburg

rmstadt

Wurzburg

C Z E C H O S L O V A K I A

Mannheim

Nuremberg

Heilronn

Karlsruhe

Treuchtlingen

Regensburg (aircraft)

Stuttgart

Koreuburg

Moosbierbaum

Floridsdoft

Ulm

Freiham

Vienna

Strasshof

Augsburg
(aircraft)

Munich

Munich

Schwechat

Lobau

Pasing

Linz

Rosenheim

Salzburg

Wiener Neustadt
(aircraft)

Friedrichshafen

A U S T R I A

Ploesti →

Dec 1943/March 1844: Mustang range, over 600 miles

Nov 1943: Lightning range, 520 miles

toeholds that were not as large as originally planned, but were nevertheless comfortable. This division had encountered the most determined German resistance of the day, together with well-directed artillery fire, and had managed to secure only a small beachhead.

As the infantry and their supporting tanks began to move inland, the Allies brought up the sections of two large artificial "Mulberry" harbors that were assembled off the British "Gold" and American "Omaha" beaches to provide

facilities for rapid disembarkation. These harbors proved invaluable in the days to come, but the American "Mulberry" was destroyed by a great storm on June 19.

Field Marshals Gerd von Rundstedt and Erwin Rommel, commanding High Command "West" and its subordinate Army Group "B" respectively, at first thought that the operation was an Allied feint. They soon revised their opinions and understood that this was the Allies' main effort. Hitler remained convinced that it was only a diversion to draw German strength away from the Pas-de-

Though the flamethrower was a terrible weapon in its effects, it was extensively used for attacks on ''hard'' targets such as strongpoints.

Opposite Top: Part of the huge Allied invasion convoy on its way to Normandy.

Opposite Bottom: DUKW amphibious trucks provided an essential link between transports lying offshore and formations already on the beachhead.

Calais, where he still expected the main Allied landing. Thus, von Rundstedt and Rommel were greatly hampered first by the slow release of reinforcements to them, and then by the slower arrival of these forces over road and railroad routes that had been devastated by months of Allied air attacks.

Even so, the German forces in the area soon recovered from their initial surprise and, with the arrival of local reserves, began to put up a stiffening resistance to the expansion of the Allied lodgement. They were greatly aided by the nature of the Normandy countryside, a woodland of small checkerboard fields separated by hedges on earthen embankments above sunken roads. Even with the aid of special armored vehicles developed largely by the British to cope with these conditions, the Allies found it difficult to develop an advance with any momentum when they had to cut through hedges that might be, and often were, covered by Germany artillery, including powerful anti-tank weapons.

The centers of the German defense were Caen in the British sector and Carentan in the American sector. The Allies closed up against these focal points by June 12 in a series of bitterly fought

Left: Operation "Overlord" was the greatest amphibious landing in history. As soon as the assault waves had moved inland and cleared the beaches, reinforcements and heavy equipment began to flood in from the Allies' vast transport fleet.

Below: The German beach defenses in Normandy, known as "Rommel's asparagus," were not particularly effective. In many places, the motion of the sea turned the obstacles around, or rolled them away, or covered them with sand. In other places, Allied demolition teams destroyed them. Also, the obstacles were located comparatively high on the beach because the German navy insisted that any invasion would be launched at high tide, when the obstacles would rip the bottoms out of landing craft. In fact, the invasion was launched at low tide, and after the landing craft had beached below them, the invading troops used the obstacles as cover.

Right: In the leading wave of the 4th Infantry Division's landing on "Utah" Beach at the extreme western end of the Allied invasion was the 8th Infantry Regiment. This photograph shows men of the regiment sheltering under the lee of a sea wall as others advance over the crest of the dune just inland of the beach itself.

Below: Reinforcements passing through "Utah" Beach on June 8, 1944. Also visible is a piece of heavy artillery, two tracked cranes, and a number of DUKW amphibious trucks. The DUKW, standardized in October 1942, was a 6 x 6 General Motors 2·5-ton truck chassis fitted with a boat hull, rudder, and propeller for waterborne capability. More than 21,000 of these vehicles were built before the end of the war, and despite their low waterborne freeboard of only some 1 foot 6 inches, these vehicles proved immensely successful. The DUKW was 31 feet long and 8 feet wide. Its maximum weight of 18,600 pounds could carry 25 troops, or 12 stretchers, or 5,000 pounds of freight. Two DUKWs yoked by a removable platform could carry a light vehicle. Powered by a gasoline engine, it was capable of 50 miles per hour on land or 5·5 knots on water.

Two Vought OS2U "Kingfisher" float planes warm up on U.S.S. *Quincy* during the Normandy landings.

engagements. By this time, the Allied lodgement contained 16 divisions.

Slow Progress

Montgomery's efforts to take Caen on June 13 and 18 were driven back, but Carentan fell to VII Corps on June 11. V and XIX Corps then fought an aggressive defense to the east, where they were joined by VIII Corps on June 15. VII Corps then drove across the base of the Cotentin peninsula to reach Carteret and Portbail on its western side on June 17. The corps then wheeled north against Cherbourg, whose major port was essential to the development of Allied strength in France. The corps had closed up around Cherbourg by June 21, but it took six days to take the city from the German defenders, who fought with great determination and finally demolished much of the harbor. Unloading was possible on the beaches almost immediately, but it was August 7 before the harbor once more became usable.

Between June 13 and 30, the Germans' chance to defeat the Allies and destroy their lodgement steadily evaporated. At Hitler's insistence, von Rundstedt began to mass the available German armor south of Caen on June 16, first to check the British and then to drive on to the coast. Montgomery's attacks forced the German commander-in-chief to commit his divisions piecemeal, however, and no decisive strength was built up. Montgomery had by this time abandoned his idea of taking Caen as the means of cutting German communications to the east. He decided instead to threaten the town in a way that made his forces a "honeypot" that would attract the weight of the German counterattacks and leave the Americans with a much easier task to the west.

A New German Commander

As early as June 17, von Rundstedt and Rommel saw the futility of the "hold

U.S. Airforce, Waist Gunner, 1944

This gunner, who is manning the trainable 0·5-inch (12·7-mm) caliber Browning heavy machine gun in one of the two waist positions of a Boeing B-17 Flying Fortress heavy bomber during daylight penetration raids to targets in Northwest Europe, was faced with the twin problems of keeping as mobile and warm as possible. Keeping warm was very difficult as he was standing just inside a hatch open to the slipstream of a bomber flying at more than 250 mph (404 km/h). As this gunner is not wearing his oxygen mask, this mission is clearly being undertaken at a lower, and therefore warmer, altitude. The parachute harness was worn at all times, and the parachute was itself stowed nearby so that it could be seized and clipped on with minimum delay should the situation demand its use.

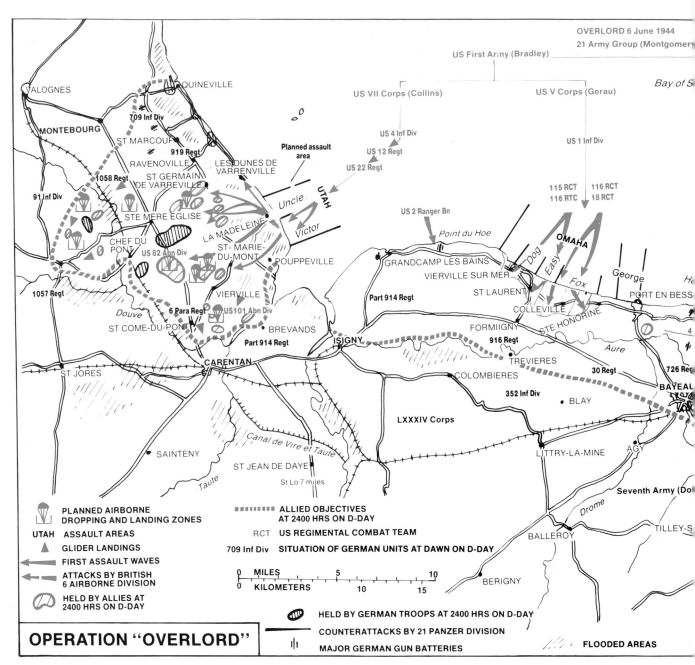

OVERLORD 6 June 1944
21 Army Group (Montgomery)
US First Army (Bradley)
US VII Corps (Collins)
US V Corps (Gerau)
Bay of S
US 4 Inf Div
US 12 Regt
US 22 Regt
US 1 Inf Div
115 RCT   116 RCT
116 RTC   18 RCT
US 2 Ranger Bn
Point du Hoe
OMAHA
GRANDCAMP LES BAINS
VIERVILLE SUR MER
ST LAURENT
Dog
Easy
Fox
George
PORT EN BESS
COLLEVILLE
STE HONORINE
FORMIIGNY
Part 914 Regt
916 Regt
Aure
TREVIERES
30 Regt
726 Reg
BAYEAU
COLOMBIERES
BLAY
352 Inf Div
LXXXIV Corps
LITTRY-LA-MINE
AGY
Canal de Vire et Taute
SAINTENY
ST JEAN DE DAYE
St Lo 7 miles
Taute
Seventh Army (Do
Drome
TILLEY-S
BALLEROY
BERIGNY

VALOGNES
QUINEVILLE
709 Inf Div
MONTEBOURG
ST MARCOUF
919 Regt
RAVENOVILLE
LES DUNES DE VARRENVILLE
ST GERMAIN DE VARREVILLE
1058 Regt
Planned assault area
91 Inf Div
STE MERE EGLISE
UTAH
Uncle
LA MADELEINE
Victor
CHEF DU PONT
US 82 Abn Div
ST-MARIE-DU-MONT
POUPPEVILLE
1057 Regt
VIERVILLE
Douve
6 Para Regt   US101 Abn Div
ST COME-DU-PONT
BREVANDS
Part 914 Regt
ISIGNY
CARENTAN
ST JORES

PLANNED AIRBORNE DROPPING AND LANDING ZONES

UTAH ASSAULT AREAS

▲ GLIDER LANDINGS

FIRST ASSAULT WAVES

ATTACKS BY BRITISH 6 AIRBORNE DIVISION

HELD BY ALLIES AT 2400 HRS ON D-DAY

ALLIED OBJECTIVES AT 2400 HRS ON D-DAY

RCT US REGIMENTAL COMBAT TEAM

709 Inf Div SITUATION OF GERMAN UNITS AT DAWN ON D-DAY

MILES   0   5   10
KILOMETERS   0   10   15

HELD BY GERMAN TROOPS AT 2400 HRS ON D-DAY

COUNTERATTACKS BY 21 PANZER DIVISION

MAJOR GERMAN GUN BATTERIES

FLOODED AREAS

OPERATION "OVERLORD"

Gunther von Kluge
For further references
see pages
90, 091, 94, 96

at all costs" tactics ordered by Hitler and asked in vain for permission to fall back. So the battle continued until the end of the month, with the Germans steadily losing strength as the Allies grew stronger day by day. On July 3, Hitler replaced von Rundstedt with Field Marshal Gunther von Kluge, who also assumed Rommel's responsibilities when the latter was wounded on July 17.

In the period between July 1 and 24, the Allied strength in Normandy grew to about a million men, 150,000 vehicles,

and 500,000 tons of supplies. This vast strength allowed the Allies to continue their program of territorial expansion, but the pace was slow. The reason was partly the nature of the country, and partly the still-powerful German defense. Against the British 2nd Army, the Germans now had the seven Panzer and two infantry divisions of General Heinz Eberbach's German Panzer Group "West," and against the 1st Army, the seven veteran infantry divisions of SS General Paul Hausser's German 7th Army.

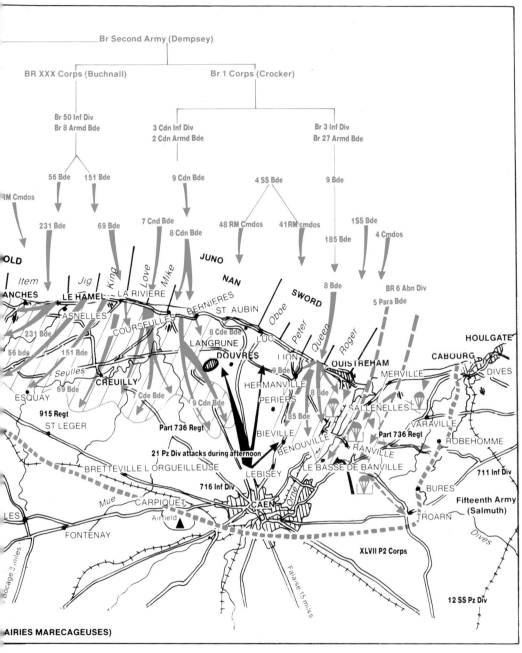

"Overlord" was a well-planned, if costly, operation. Its success, coupled with the westward offensives launched by the huge Soviet army groups, paved the way for the Allied liberation of northwestern Europe and the crushing of Germany.

As the placement of the German armor suggests, Montgomery's ploy was working well in drawing the Germans' main strength against the British. It is hardly surprising, therefore, that the British 2nd Army made slow and costly progress, though it did finally take the western part of Caen on July 8. On July 18, it took the eastern part of the town, at the beginning of an offensive that was finally halted on July 20 after the British 2nd Army had established a line running in an arc around the southeastern side of the city.

The Fight for Saint Lo

The Germans' concentration on the British effort to take Caen provided Bradley with the chance he needed to expand the American sector. On July 18, Saint Lo fell to the divisions of XIX and VII Corps, whose five divisions suffered 11,000 casualties during the 12 days of their attack. American possession of this key point on the southwestern corner of the lodgement allowed the line west of it

Above Left: A U.S. mortar crew in action during the fighting around Saint Lo. Such weapons provided ideal short-range support fire for infantry. The mortar bombs were lobbed high into the air to fall vertically onto the enemy.

Left: G.I.s receive a French welcome in Saint Lo after the decisive breakout in Operation "Cobra." This action paved the way for the American push out of the Normandy lodgement toward Avranches and the classic pursuit of the new 3rd Army east across central France.

Left: A convoy of American trucks grinds through Saint Lo, which was almost totally destroyed in the fighting.

Below: An American patrol picks its way through the ruins of Saint Lo. The Germans had a well-deserved reputation for superb holding action in such conditions, and advancing Allied infantry were always wary of ruins.

to be straightened, and by July 24, VIII Corps had pushed south to a line running between Saint Lo and Lessay on the western side of the Cotentin peninsula, though Bradley had wanted VII Corps to reach Coutances, even farther south.

At this point, the first phase of the invasion was complete. It had taken considerably longer than expected and had cost the Allies 122,000 casualties, to German losses of 114,000 that included 41,000 men taken prisoner.

With the main German strength concentrated against the British 2nd Army, the situation was now ripe for the breakout that Montgomery had long wanted and Eisenhower had recently come to accept. The Allied situation was eased by the availability of substantial forces, for, although the Normandy lodgement on July 24 (48 days after D-Day) covered only the area planned for the fifth day after the invasion, the build-up of men and equipment had continued at the originally planned rate. There had been shortages of ammunition and antitank guns capable of dealing with the latest German armor, but these difficulties were being overcome, and manpower replacements more than exceeded casualties.

Operation "Cobra"

Launched on July 25, Operation "Cobra" threw the 1st Army against the German 7th Army west of Saint Lo in an offensive that was designed with the limited objective of extending the lodgement south to Coutances. The countryside here was thought suitable for the eventual breakout from the lodgement, which was planned as a massive leftward wheeling movement, pivoting on Caumont, to the south and southeast. The 1st Army's main blow was to be struck by VII Corps with three infantry, two armored, and one motorized divisions after a path had been blown through the German defenses by the corps' own reinforced artillery strength and a "bomb carpet." This fearsome tactic, measuring 2,500 yards by 6,000 yards, was created by 4,200 tons of bombs dropped by heavy and medium bombers, supplemented by fighter bombers.

The infantry were to attack right behind the bombs and break through whatever might be left of the German defenses, allowing the three other divisions to pass through the gap in the German line without hindrance. The motorized infantry division was to seize Coutances, and of the armored divisions, one was to envelop the town from the south as the other plunged south to block all approach routes between Tessy on the Vire River and Villedieu on the Sienne River.

On VII Corps' right, Middleton's VIII Corps would attack after the capture of Coutances and, moving south, complete the encirclement of the German LXXXIV Corps. On VII Corps' left, Major General Charles H. Corlett's XIX Corps, supported still farther to the east by V Corps, would pin the German II Parachute Corps down and prevent its movement to the west.

It was now that Montgomery's Caen "honeypot" came into its own. Like Hitler, von Kluge had come to accept

that the threat posed by the British 2nd Army was greater than anything the 1st Army might offer, and he had therefore virtually ignored the needs of the German 7th Army as he tried to establish a mobile, if not fully armored, reserve near Caen. The German 7th Army therefore lacked strength and could not deploy in depth. Of the 30,000 Germans facing VII Corps on July 24, only about 5,000 (mainly from the Panzer Lehr Division) were in the front line.

Even though some of the bombs fell short and caused 558 American casualties, the bomb carpet proved remarkably successful, virtually wiping out the Panzer Lehr Division and so shocking the surviving men that no effective resistance was offered as the three infantry divisions swept forward. Good progress was made during the day, at the cost of 1,060 casualties as the Germans finally recovered and started to fight back. Collins realized the importance of maintaining the momentum of the advance and, gambling that the Germans had little more to throw into the battle, he committed his two mobile forces on July 26.

The eastern mobile force met virtually no resistance and passed through Marigny to approach Tessy on July 27. Here it was taken under command by XIX Corps, and during the next three days, the Americans fought back determined German attacks on VII Corps' left flank. Von

The pace and scope of Allied bombing efforts reached a crescendo in 1944. Although much of Germany's fighter capability had been destroyed, American bombers were still lost or damaged. Here, an airman examines damage to the tail of a Consolidated B-24 Liberator bomber after returning to its English base.

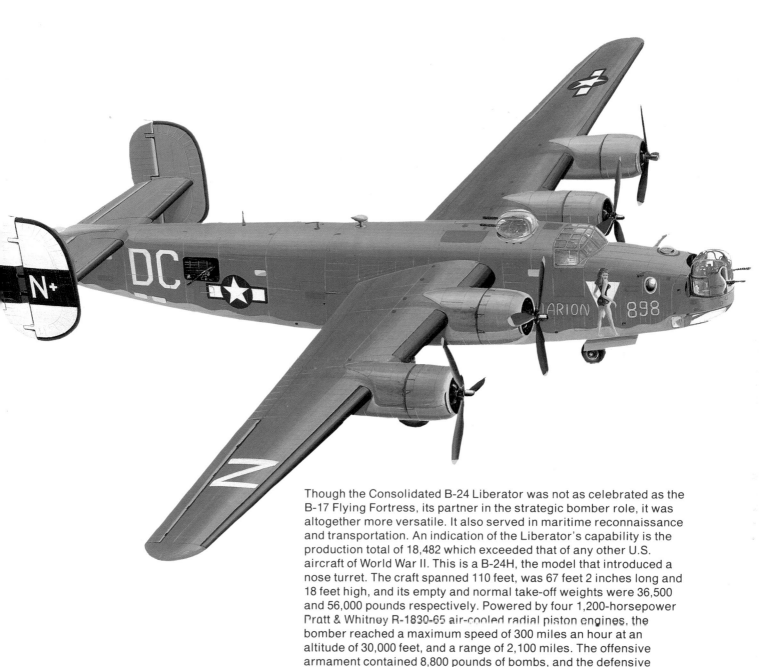

Though the Consolidated B-24 Liberator was not as celebrated as the B-17 Flying Fortress, its partner in the strategic bomber role, it was altogether more versatile. It also served in maritime reconnaissance and transportation. An indication of the Liberator's capability is the production total of 18,482 which exceeded that of any other U.S. aircraft of World War II. This is a B-24H, the model that introduced a nose turret. The craft spanned 110 feet, was 67 feet 2 inches long and 18 feet high, and its empty and normal take-off weights were 36,500 and 56,000 pounds respectively. Powered by four 1,200-horsepower Pratt & Whitney R-1830-65 air-cooled radial piston engines, the bomber reached a maximum speed of 300 miles an hour at an altitude of 30,000 feet, and a range of 2,100 miles. The offensive armament contained 8,800 pounds of bombs, and the defensive armament included ten 0·5-inch machine guns in twin-gun tail, dorsal, ventral, and nose turrets, and single-gun waist positions. The crew was between eight and 12.

Kluge had suddenly appreciated the danger presented by "Cobra" on July 27, and he sent two Panzer divisions to the 7th Army. On the same day, von Kluge finally received permission from Hitler to draw on forces in the Pas-de-Calais region in an effort to stabilize the deteriorating situation in Normandy.

The western mobile force met strong German resistance as it moved on Coutances, and it lost the speed it needed to secure this target without delay. The objective was reassigned to VIII Corps on July 27. The Germans managed to hold open a corridor down the coast, allowing most of LXXXIV Corps to escape. But then Hausser ordered this formation to move not south but east, where it ran into

91

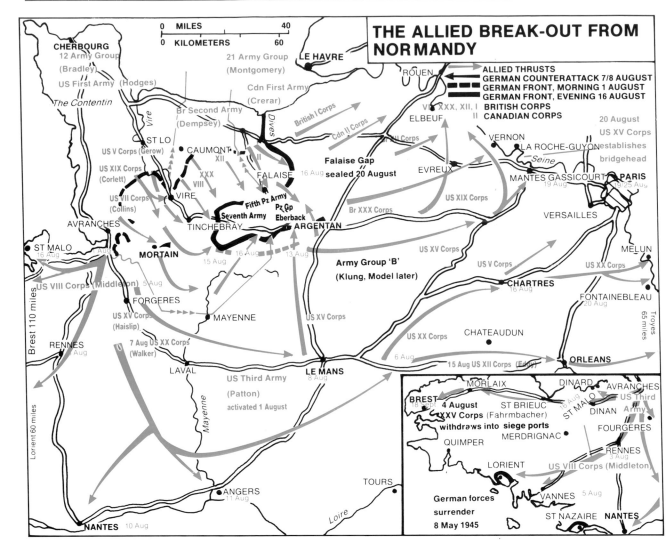

A Limited Attack Becomes a Full Offensive

With the situation developing even better than he and Collins had hoped, Bradley ordered a full exploitation on July 28, and this limited operation became a major offensive in its own right. Avranches fell on July 30, and the Americans were perfectly positioned for a development to the east and southeast. This move would decisively sever the German 7th Army from the German 1st Army in southwest France and open a host of strategic possibilities in the rear of Army Group "B."

It had been decided earlier that, when the American breakout came, a corps would be detached into Brittany. Here lay ports such as Saint Malo, Brest, Lorient, and Saint Nazaire, which were considered essential for the development of the Allies' full strength in France, but which were strongly held by determined German formations. VIII Corps was selected for this transfer and came under the command of Lieutenant General Patton's 3rd Army, which became operational on August 1. On the same day, the 12th Army Group was formed under Bradley to control the two American armies in northwestern France, and command of the 1st Army passed to Lieutenant General Courtney H. Hodges. Montgomery retained overall control of the ground forces, whose British 21st Army Group now included the new Canadian 1st Army.

The American breakout from Normandy past Saint Lo was greatly helped by the fact that the main German strength had been drawn to the east by British attacks around Caen.

Enter Patton and the 3rd Army

The 3rd Army was entrusted with the task of plunging deep into France along the northern side of the Loire River, but was initially hampered by the transportation bottleneck at Avranches. While engineers remedied the situation, the aggressive Patton fanned VIII Corps into Brittany, where the 83rd Infantry Division took Saint Malo under siege on August 3, the 8th Infantry Division took Rennnes on the same day, and the 4th and 6th Armored Divisions respectively invested Lorient and Brest on August 7. Saint Malo was captured on August 17 and Brest surrendered on September 18, but Lorient and Saint Nazaire held out until the end of the war, surrendering only on May 8, 1945. This did not worry the Allies unduly, since the Brittany ports were found to be unnecessary after Cherbourg and Marseille had been prepared to work at full capacity.

As VIII Corps swept through Brittany, Patton was getting the rest of his army on the move. The first of these formations was Major General Walton H. Walker's XX Corps, which was joined on its right during August 7 by Major General Wade H. Haislip's XV Corps, and finally on their right during August 15 by Major General Manton S. Eddy's XII Corps. XX Corps initially drove straight south to reach Nantes and Angers on the Loire River on August 10 and 11 respectively, and then

Below: The German armor most feared by the Allies in northwestern France included the Panzerkampfwagen V Panther and PzKpfw VI Tiger. This tank graveyard at Isigny in northern France contains examples of both types. The vehicle numbered 425 is a Panther, which was armed with a high-velocity 75-mm gun and possessed formidable protection and mobility. Vehicle number 898 is a Tiger, which was armed with an 88-mm gun, and had very thick armor, but was also very slow. The Tiger's gun was derived from the celebrated 88-mm antiaircraft and antitank gun. Firing its powerful projectile at a very high velocity, it was more than a match for any American tank of the period.

wheeled east, parallel to the line of the river. The other two corps came into action on XX Corps' left and moved first southeast and then east in a fast-moving offensive that found them spread out in an arc between Argentan on the Dives River and Angers by August 13, with the farthest units well to the southeast of Le Mans.

On the 3rd Army's left, the 1st Army's V, XIX, and VII Corps were wheeling left on a shorter radius toward Argentan. Initially, the 1st Army had to stop an ill-considered but determined counterattack at Mortain by reinforced elements of the German 7th Army. This action had been ordered by Hitler to try to drive through from Mortain to the coast near Avranches. Success would have cut off the 3rd Army and then, in Hitler's fevered imagination, allow his 7th Army to turn north to destroy the Normandy lodgement. The offensive began on August 6 and fell first on the 30th Infantry Division of VII Corps. The division fell back, but Collins threw the rest of his corps into the battle and Bradley brought in reinforcements that, with the aid of British air power, halted the German thrust by August 8. Against von Kluge's advice,

Hitler insisted that the Germans fight on for another two days, though the only real results were additional Germans losses.

The Battle of the Falaise Gap

All this while, a noose of Allied forces was closing around three major German

forces (the German 5th Panzer Army, 7th Army, and Panzer Group "Eberbach"). In the north and west, these units were pinned by four corps of the Canadian 1st and British 2nd Armies; in the south, they were being compressed by VII and V Corps of the 1st Army; and in the southeast, the advancing XV Corps of the 3rd Army threatened to seal the neck of the Allied bottle enclosing these German forces. It was a position of immense potential importance to the Allies, but on August 13, Bradley ordered XV Corps to halt because he feared that the Allied

forces might get mixed up and fire on each other.

The following day, Bradley clearly believed that the attempt to trap German forces in the Falaise-Argentan pocket had failed and ordered Patton to send two of XV Corps' divisions east toward Dreux. Montgomery had ordered on August 11 that, if the encirclement failed, a wider enveloping movement was to be attempted. With hindsight, it is possible to see that Bradley misread a difficult situation, for the Falaise-Argentan pocket was in fact close to completion, with

American and Canadian troops separated by only about ten miles. Von Kluge thought the situation was so desperate that he asked Hitler to authorize an immediate withdrawal, and permission was given on August 16. The following day, Hitler ordered Field Marshal Walther Model from the Eastern Front to replace von Kluge, which he did on August 25.

The three almost trapped German formations were assaulted on their flanks by Allied ground forces and from all directions by Allied fighter bombers, including R.A.F. rocket-firing Hawker Typhoons which caused terrible devastation. The weary soldiers streamed east as the noose continued to tighten. By the end of the day on August 19, the remaining Germans held a small pocket just north of Argentan. They continued to escape through the narrow gap between Saint Lambert and Saint Leonard until the break was closed as the Poles of the Canadian 1st Army and Americans of the 3rd Army met at Chambois. The battle of the Falaise-Argentan gap cost the 1st Army 19,000 casualties and the 3rd Army about 10,000 more, but the Germans lost about 50,000 captured, 10,000 dead, and very large numbers of armored and other vehicles destroyed or abandoned. Even so,

substantial numbers of men and armored vehicles had managed to escape.

The 3rd Army Streams East

The rest of the 3rd Army had meanwhile been fanning out to the east, between the Loire River in the south and the line from Argentan to Dreux in the north. The other three Allied armies followed on the 3rd Army's left flank as soon as they could. The Germans realized that they could not hope to check the Allies in the short term and pulled back as rapidly as they could toward the line of the Seine River. By August 25, the four Allied armies had closed up to this river line along most of its length as far to the southeast as Troyes, well up-river from Paris. The only two major areas west of the river still held by the Germans were between Rouen and the sea in the northwest, and between Fontainebleu and Troyes in the southeast.

On August 23, the population of Paris rose against the Germans as the Allies approached the French capital. Patton rushed his V Corps into the city, with the French 2nd Armored Division spearheading the thrust for political reasons.

A major part of the Allied ground forces' success in the campaigns in Normandy and northwestern France was attributable to the devastating capability of Allied tactical air power. The major American tactical air formation was the 9th Army Air Force. These Martin B-26 Marauder medium bombers are unloading their bombs on the German supply network. This meant that front-line German formations never received adequate reinforcements or supplies.

The Invasion of Southern France

By this time, the Germans were fighting a two-front war in France, for on August 15, the long-planned invasion of southern France had begun. This diversionary operation, codenamed "Anvil," had been proposed by the CCS in August 1943 as a prelude to "Overlord" and was confirmed at the Tehran Conference. The size and longer-term objectives of "Anvil" could not be finalized because of the logistical demands of "Overlord" and the continued operations in Italy. Therefore, the Allies decided to launch this invasion after "Overlord," instead of before, to allow all available amphibious capability to be allocated to the more important "Overlord."

In late July, at almost exactly the same time that the Allied forces were breaking out of their lodgement in Normandy, it seemed that great success was just around the corner in Italy. The British questioned the continued need for "Anvil," arguing that the forces earmarked for the invasion of southern France would be better employed in Italy, where the British wanted to develop the Allies' expected success against the "Gothic" Line into a drive through to western Austria.

Generals Marshall and Eisenhower were still sure that "Anvil" was vital to provide flank support for the "Overlord" forces and to secure Marseille as a major

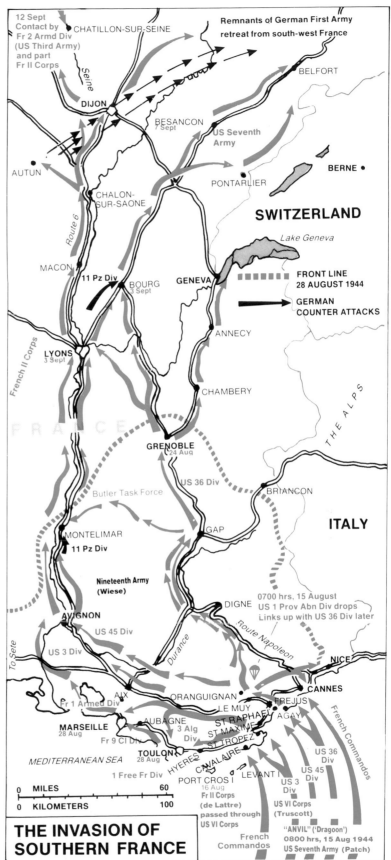

THE INVASION OF SOUTHERN FRANCE

Allied supply port. The dispute was finally taken to Roosevelt and Churchill, who decided in favor of the American position and ordered the implementation of what now became Operation "Dragoon," with American and French forces drawn from Italy and North Africa.

The formation tasked with the operation was Lieutenant General Alexander M. Patch's 7th Army, which included Truscott's VI Corps, the French II Corps, and two specialist organizations, the 1st Airborne Task Force and the 1st Special Service Force. The latter was an American-Canadian brigade that had originally been raised for service against the Japanese in the Aleutian Islands off Alaska, but which had been deployed to the Italian theater instead. Naval and air support was entrusted to Vice Admiral Hewitt's Western Task Force and the U.S. Army Air Forces' XII Tactical Air Command in Corsica, supported by the heavy bombers of the 15th Army Air Force in Italy.

This formidable grouping was opposed by General Friedrich Wiese's German 19th Army, whose eight divisions included only one first-line formation, the 11th Panzer Division.

Operation "Dragoon"

The invasion was preceded by naval demonstrations near Nice and Marseille, east and west of the chosen assault area, and by a diversionary airborne invasion using explosive-filled dummies. Then French commandos landed to block the coastal highway east and west of the assault area, and the 1st SSF took the islands of Fort Cros and Levant to destroy the gun batteries, which turned out to be German decoys. The landing, scheduled for the morning of August 15, was opened by a very successful airborne drop near Oraguignan. The men and machines of VI Corps' three infantry divisions were supported by massive air and naval bombardments, and they landed without serious opposition except in the area of the 36th Infantry Division near Saint Raphael on the right of the assault.

By nightfall, some 94,000 men and more than 11,000 vehicles had landed, and by midday on August 17, the troops had broken the two German second-line divisions in the area and passed beyond the original beachhead line. The French II

A poignant image: a M10 tank destroyer roars past a French memorial for the dead of the previous world war.

Opposite Top: A paratrooper sergeant models his full jump kit, complete with two parachutes (main canopy on the back and emergency canopy on the front), map case, a knife, and various satchels.

Above: American infantry land from their LCVPs in the south of France during Operation "Anvil." This well-executed operation, involving American and French forces, opened the way for the capture of Marseille as the Americans surged north up the valley of the Rhone River. Marseille was soon in operation as a major Allied supply port.

Right: A scene typical of loading operations at many ports, which for VI Corps included Naples and Salerno in southern Italy, prior to Operation "Anvil."

Corps began to land after VI Corps and passed through the left-hand American formations to advance west on Toulon and Marseille as the Americans pushed northwest toward the Durance River.

The German 19th Army Escapes

Toulon and Marseille were French objectives. Both were captured on August 28, and Marseille was opened to Allied shipping on September 15. Meanwhile, VI Corps split into two main columns with the 36th Infantry Division on the right and the 3rd and 45th Infantry Divisions on the left. The right-hand column moved up the Durance River and then advanced via Gap toward Grenoble, which it entered on August 24. The left-hand column moved into the valley of the Rhone River at Avignon and advanced north in pursuit of the fleeing German 19th Army. Patch hoped to trap the German formation by cutting its line of retreat at Montelimar with the specially created Task Force "Butler" of the 36th Infantry Division. This move failed because it took the task force too long to cut across to the west from Gap, and the German 19th Army managed to pull back to the north after 57,000 men were taken prisoner. The

left-hand column entered Lyon on September 3; the same day, advance detachments of the two columns met at Bourg.

At Lyon, the left-hand column of VI Corps veered toward the northeast in the direction of Besancon and the Belfort gap. The French II Corps had paralleled the course of VI Corps on the western side of the Rhone River. Now they continued north up the line of the Saone River toward Dijon and then down the upper reaches of the Seine River to make contact with the French 2nd Armored Division and lead the 3rd Army advance in this sector on September 12.

The 6th Army Group Is Created

On September 15, the "Dragoon" forces – the 7th Army and the newly formed French 1st Army – became Lieutenant General Jacob M. Devers's 6th Army Group. By this time, the Americans and the French in this region had reached the Vosges region.

During this same period, the 12th and British 21st Army Groups had burst over the Seine River above and below Paris. Protected on their otherwise exposed southern flank along the line of the Loire River by Lieutenant General William

Opposite Top: The Franco-American landing in southern France played havoc with Allied operations in Italy. The formations available in that area were reduced, and supply traffic was disrupted as units moved away from the Italian front toward the ports where they were to embark for the southern French landing. These M4 Sherman medium tanks are on the last lap of their transit to an Italian port.

Opposite Bottom: An American force halts on the road near Epernay on the upper part of the Marne River to engage a German target.

Boeing B-17F Flying Fortress bombers of the 8th Army Air Force are seen on their way to a target in Europe.

H. Simpson's 9th Army, which became operational on September 5, the Allies' northern armies flooded forward to the northeast and east.

In May 1944, SHAEF had fixed the Ruhr industrial region between Dusseldorf and Essen as the Allies' first objective in Germany. The primary advance would therefore move through Amiens and Liege, shielded on its southern flank by a secondary advance toward Verdun and Metz. There had been suggestions for a single massive advance on Germany, but they were discounted because such an operation could have been channeled by the Germans and then destroyed by concentrated counteroffensives.

Revised Allied Plan

On August 19, as the Allies approached the line of the Seine River, the plan was revised. The situation had altered radically since the original scheme had been worked out in May: Germany had lost 530,000 men defending Normandy, the German 5th Panzer and German 7th Armies had virtually ceased to exist, and only about 120 German tanks had regained the eastern bank of the Seine River. Montgomery and Bradley urged Eisenhower to allow a single main thrust

The airborne part of Operation "Anvil" was the most successful paratroop drop of the war, and American paratroopers were soon involved in the campaign as ordinary infantrymen. These paratroopers are waiting in a ditch near La Motte for the order to move up.

into Germany, with each suggesting his own group to lead the operation. Eisenhower, however, reverted to the essence of the May plan and ordered Bradley to support Montgomery with Hodges's 1st Army. Bradley was unhappy with this decision, but Patton was even unhappier: his 3rd Army would have to make do with the supplies and fuel left after the 1st Army's needs had been filled.

Pursuit from the Seine River

The general offensive east and northeast from the line of the Seine River began on August 26, when the 3rd Army smashed forward and managed to cross the Meuse River on August 30 before being halted by lack of fuel. The 1st Army swung into action on August 27 and by September 3 had reached Mons, capturing 25,000 Germans in the process. On the 1st Army's left, the British 2nd Army attacked on August 29 and by September 3 had moved into Brussels, the capital of Belgium. The Canadian 1st Army had the most difficult and least glamorous task; they advanced along the southern coast of the English Channel investing the strongly garrisoned ports of Le Havre, Dieppe, Boulogne, Calais, and Dunkirk. The first four fell between September 12 and 30.

The most crucial day in this period for the Germans was September 4, when the British 2nd Army captured Antwerp before the Germans could demolish its large port facilities. This opened the very real possibility that the Allies could use Antwerp as their main supply port. The Germans responded with speed, sending Colonel General Kurt Student's 1st Parachute Army to hold the line of the Antwerp Canal in Belgium. At the same time, General Gustav von Zangen's 15th Army was ordered to hold the northern side of the Schelde River estuary to cut the Allies off from the river, which was the sole approach to the port of Antwerp. On September 5, von Rundstedt was recalled to head High Command "West."

Eisenhower Takes Command

It had meanwhile become clear that the control of the three Allied armies in France meant that SHAEF needed to be there. On September 3, Eisenhower assumed operational control of all the Allied land forces. Eisenhower had by now recognized the strategic value of Patton's position, and he authorized the 3rd Army to press its advance, with the 1st Army shifted from northeast to east as its left-flank guard. By September 14, the 3rd Army had reached the line of the

DUKWs land under fire during Operation "Dragoon."

Moselle River as far south as Epinal, and the 1st Army had reached the German border between Aachen and Trier.

Montgomery was still adamant that he could reach the Ruhr if he had adequate support and supplies. Eisenhower, stressing the importance of clearing the Schelde River estuary so that Antwerp could become the main Allied supply port, gave the British 21st Army Group priority to receive supplies. At the same time, he refused to halt the diverging attacks of the 1st and 3rd Armies.

The main problem facing the Allies was that, since their breakout from Normandy, they had moved considerably ahead of their schedule of advance and created for themselves a logistical

Below: While the main part of the 12th Army Group moved east through France after the break-out from Normandy, VIII corps was left in Brittany to besiege and take the ports of northwestern France held by the German XXV Corps. This 105-mm M3 howitzer is in action against the German defenders of Brest, which fell on September 18. The weapon's most unusual feature was its axle, which could be rotated upward through 180° to lift the wheels off the ground and so lower the piece onto a stable firing platform. This M3 is being fired on its wheels. The weapon weighed 2,495 pounds and fired its 33-pound HE projectile to a maximum range of 7,250 yards.

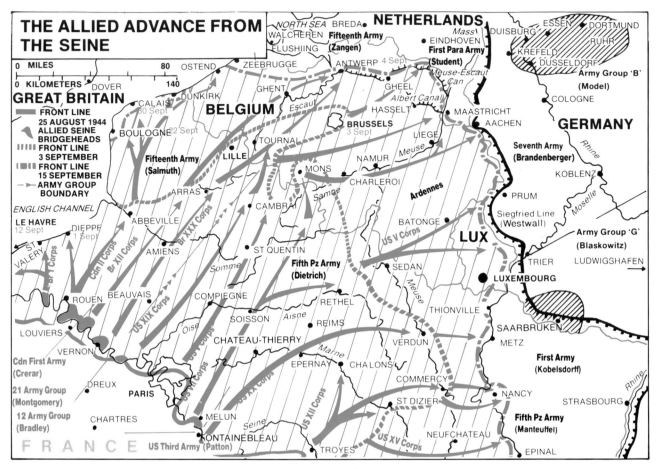

THE ALLIED ADVANCE FROM THE SEINE

0 MILES 80
0 KILOMETERS 140

GREAT BRITAIN

FRONT LINE 25 AUGUST 1944
ALLIED SEINE BRIDGEHEADS
FRONT LINE 3 SEPTEMBER
FRONT LINE 15 SEPTEMBER
ARMY GROUP BOUNDARY

ENGLISH CHANNEL

Cdn First Army (Crerar)
21 Army Group (Montgomery)
12 Army Group (Bradley)

nightmare. The reopening of ports, the relaying of railroads, the rebuilding of roads, the repair of bridges, and the creation of fuel pipelines had lagged far behind the progress of the front-line formations, which therefore found themselves short of all essential supplies.

The Arnhem Gamble

The 6th and 12th Army Groups were now struggling against a shortage of supplies more than against the Germans. As they inched toward the "Westwall," or "Siegfried" Line, the much vaunted but obsolete line of fixed defenses guarding Germany's western frontier, Montgomery suggested a bold gamble. Success would put his British 2nd Army in a position outflanking the northern end of the German defenses.

His plan was a combined offensive in which Operation "Market" would land the three airborne divisions of Lieutenant General Lewis H. Brereton's Allied 1st

Airborne Army behind the German lines. They would take the bridges over five waterways, including three rivers, as stepping stones on the road causeway through marshy ground. This would then be the 65-mile line of advance for Operation "Garden," in which the mechanized and motorized forces of the British 2nd Army's XXX Corps would punch their way to Arnhem over the "airborne carpet" to try to turn the northern flank of the Westwall.

The operation began on September 17, and the two American divisions of Major General Ridgway's XVIII Airborne Corps were tasked with taking and holding the first four of the five main bridges. The two bridges nearest XXX Corps' starting line were those over the Wilhelmina Canal at Zon and over the Zuit Willemsvaart Canal at Veghel. Both were taken by Taylor's 101st Airborne Division on the first day, for relief by XXX Corps during the afternoon of the following day. Next were the bridges over the Maas River at Grave and over the Waal River at Nijmegen. They

The broad front of the Allied advance from the Seine River into Belgium and eastern France opened a number of strategic possibilities for continued operations against the German armies.

Left: After its liberation, Paris was thought to be a possible target for German air attack, so limited air defenses were established. Among them was this position on a bridge leading into the Place de la Concorde.

Below: The truly international nature of the Allied effort against Germany is highlighted in this photograph of American and Free French troops in a joint parade.

were the objectives of Ridgway's own 82nd Airborne Division, which took the Grave Bridge during the afternoon of September 17 and was relieved by XXX Corps during the morning of September 18. The Nijmegen bridge proved more troublesome and was not fully taken by the 82nd Airborne Division and XXX Corps until September 20.

German resistance was strengthening all the time, and in Arnhem, the British 1st Airborne Division managed to take only the northern end of the bridge over the Lek River. Elements of the division held out with great gallantry against overwhelming odds, but XXX Corps could not break through to them, and on September 25/26, the surviving British surrendered or escaped across the river to reach XXX Corps on the southern bank.

Montgomery's gamble had failed, and there was now no alternative to a headlong attack on the Westwall by the 12th Army Group and the clearance of the Schelde estuary by the British 21st Army Group. Some very bitter fighting took

place on the estuary between October 1 and November 8, but by November 4, Allied minesweepers were at work in the estuary, and the 70-mile channel was swept 16 times by 100 Allied vessels before the first loaded convoy moved into Antwerp on November 27.

Inching Toward the Westwall

As the British and Canadians developed their position in Belgium, Eisenhower pushed his American armies forward against the Westwall from October 1 to 23. From north to south, the 12th Army Group had the 1st, 9th, and 3rd Armies in the line, and they pressed forward from a point north of Maastricht as far south as Luneville. From Luneville to the Swiss frontier, the 6th Army Group deployed the 7th and French 1st Armies. The 1st Army took Aachen on October 21 after particularly bitter fighting; the 9th Army was involved mainly in patrol activity. The 3rd Army had to defeat a German spoiling offensive before it could move forward to take Metz on October 3. It was then forced to pull back on October 17, but the 6th Army Group pushed the German forces back into the Vosges Mountains.

Above: Huge numbers of U.S. troops took part in the victory parade along the Champs Elysees after the liberation of Paris.

Right: The entertainment industry played a major part in boosting the morale of American fighting men. Here Fred Astaire stands by to give oxygen to an unhappy Bing Crosby, who is faced with the prospect of a horse-sized injection!

The hand of praise from Eisenhower for one of the many thousands of soldiers who played so important a part in keeping supplies moving to the front line. In the foreground, with lifting rings in place of their fuses, are 155-mm M101 projectiles, weighing 127 pounds, for the M1A1 ''Long Tom'' gun.

When the Allies advanced into Germany, they were amazed at the devastation of major towns and cities. This private is standing amid such ruins, with the spires of Cologne Cathedral in the background.

By the middle of October, Eisenhower saw that the British 21st Army Group was still too involved in the Belgian fighting to play any immediate part in SHAEF's planned drive to the line of the Rhine River. He therefore gave the major role to the 12th Army Group, with the 3rd Army allocated a secondary role, together with the 6th and British 21st Army Groups. On October 28, Eisenhower ordered a general offensive intended to destroy all German forces in its path and reach the Rhine River, and if possible seize bridgeheads across this main barrier to an Allied penetration into the heart of Germany. Eisenhower's thoughts were still concentrated on an early seizure of the Ruhr valley, and he therefore expected to switch the main weight of the Allied offensive back to the British 21st Army Group at a later date.

Bradley anticipated such a move and, to keep the veteran 1st Army available to his own army group, he switched the inexperienced 9th Army onto the 1st Army's left, where it bordered the British 21st Army Group and would therefore be the logical choice if any of his armies had to be detached.

The Americans Move Into the Rhineland

Preceded by the heaviest tactical bombing preparation yet seen in the west, the 9th and 1st Armies moved forward on a narrow front during November 16. The Germans fought with a grimness that appeared even more determined than before, and the two armies had a particularly hard time as they moved through the Westwall, especially in the area of the Hurtgen Forest. The offensive finally reached the Roer River. Bradley ordered that no effort should be made to secure bridgeheads across this river. Worried that the Germans would flood the Roer River valley by opening the dams near Schmidt, he ordered the 1st Army to plan their immediate capture.

Farther south, the 3rd Army had encircled Metz by November 18. The city fell on November 22, but the last of the forts around it did not surrender until December 13. Over the same period, XII and XX Corps of the 3rd Army pushed the Germans back to the Westwall, captured Sarreguemines during December 6, and had

Men of the 101st Airborne Division load a Jeep of one of the formation's medical units into the fuselage of a Waco CG-4A assault glider in preparation for Operation "Market Garden." The division's tasks were the capture of the bridges over the Wilhelmina Canal at Zon and over the Zuit Willemsvaart Canal at Veghel. The glider, towed by a Douglas C-47 Skytrain, was attached to the tow cable by a quick-release mechanism on the glider's nose.

secured several small bridgeheads across the Saar River by December 15. These gains seemed small by comparison with Patton's previous advances, but the 3rd Army was now well supplied and admirably placed to strike hard and deep into Germany.

Great Progress by the 6th Army Group

The largest advances were made by the 6th Army Group. Despite the snow and cold that had affected the operations of all the American forces, the 7th Army attacked on November 13 and reached Sarrebourg by November 20. The army was spearheaded by the French 2nd Armored Division, commanded by Major General Leclerc (whose bitter personal enmity with General de Lattre de Tassigny meant that the division never served in the latter's French 1st Army). The division now led the way as the 7th Army's XV Corps outflanked and then cleared the Saverne Gap before taking Strasbourg on

November 23. Leaving the French 1st Army to pin the Germans in the Colmar pocket between Strasbourg and the Swiss border, Devers changed the axis of the 7th Army's advance from east to northeast. By December 15, the army had closed up to the Westwall between Karlsruhe and Bitche.

Although the American offensives of November had hit the Germans hard, they had not been as successful as the Allies had hoped. It is not surprising, therefore, that Montgomery urged Eisenhower to switch the main Allied effort back to the north by resuming the original "narrow front" strategy. Eisenhower refused and ordered a continuation of the current "broad front" effort, which caused some stress in relations between the United States and the United Kingdom.

A Combined Strategy

Despite the limited success of the November offensives, Eisenhower decided that the major offensive would be resumed

Overleaf: In February and March 1945, the Allies moved up to the line of the Rhine River along virtually its entire length. They secured decisive bridgeheads that were rapidly exploited to drive armored daggers into the German heartland.

An American medical corpsman provides a wounded German soldier with first-aid treatment for a wounded shoulder.

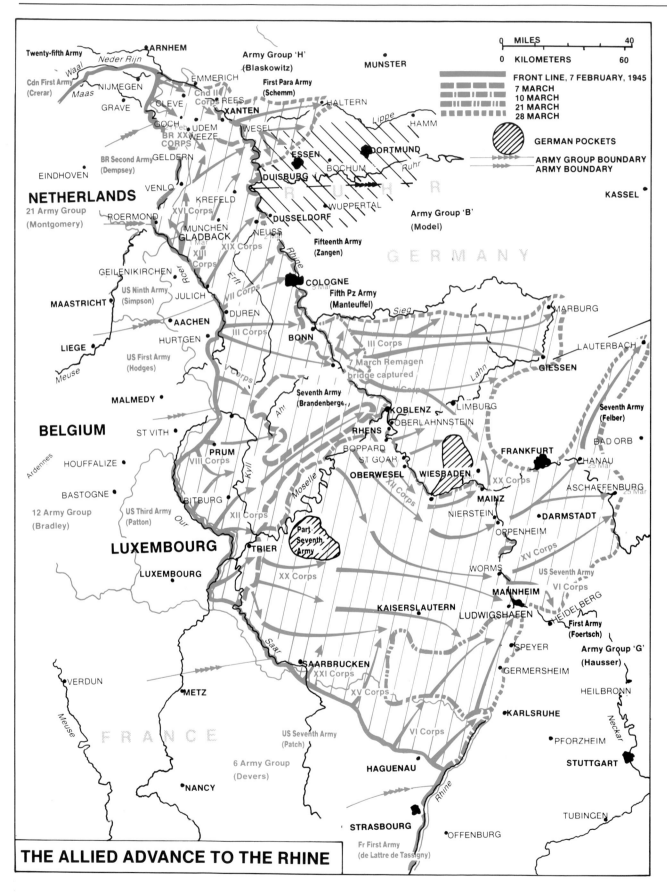

Twenty-fifth Army

Cdn First Army
(Crerar)

ARNHEM
Neder Rijn
EMMERICH
NIJMEGEN
GRAVE
CLEVE
GOCH
UDEM
BR XX
CORPS
WEEZE
GELDERN

Waal
Maas

Army Group 'H'
(Blaskowitz)

First Para Army
(Schemm)

Cnd II
Corps
REES
XANTEN
WESEL

MUNSTER

HALTERN

Lippe
HAMM

ESSEN
BOCHUM
DORTMUND
DUISBURG
Ruhr

BR Second Army
(Dempsey)

NETHERLANDS

EINDHOVEN

VENLO

KREFELD

DUSSELDORF

WUPPERTAL

KASSEL

21 Army Group
(Montgomery)

ROERMOND

XVI Corps
MUNCHEN
GLADBACK
XIII
Corps

NEUSS

Army Group 'B'
(Model)

GERMANY

GEILENIKIRCHEN

XIX Corps

Rhine

COLOGNE

Fifth Pz Army
(Manteuffel)

MARBURG

MAASTRICHT

US Ninth Army
(Simpson)

JULICH

VII Corps

Sieg

Fifteenth Army
(Zangen)

AACHEN

DUREN

III Corps

BONN

III Corps

LAUTERBACH

GIESSEN

7 March Remagen
bridge captured

Lahn

LIEGE

HURTGEN

US First Army
(Hodges)

Corps

Meuse

Seventh Army
(Brandenberge

LIMBURG

MALMEDY

Ahr

KOBLENZ
OBERLAHNNSTEIN

Seventh Army
(Felber)

BELGIUM

ST VITH

RHENS

FRANKFURT

BAD ORB

BOPPARD
ST GOAR

WIESBADEN

HANAU

HOUFFALIZE

PRUM
VIII Corps

OBERWESEL

XII Corps

ASCHAFFENBURG

Ardennes

BASTOGNE

Kyll

Moselle

MAINZ

NIERSTEIN

DARMSTADT

12 Army Group
(Bradley)

US Third Army
(Patton)

BITBURG

XII Corps

OPPENHEIM

Our

LUXEMBOURG

Part
Seventh
Army

TRIER

XV Corps

LUXEMBOURG

XX Corps

WORMS

US Seventh Army
VI Corps

MANNHEIM

KAISERSLAUTERN
LUDWIGSHAFEN

HEIDELBERG

First Army
(Foertsch)

SPEYER

Army Group 'G'
(Hausser)

METZ

SAARBRUCKEN
XXI Corps

Saar

GERMERSHEIM

HEILBRONN

VERDUN

XV Corps

Meuse

KARLSRUHE

Neckar

VI Corps

PFORZHEIM

F R A N C E

US Seventh Army
(Patch)

6 Army Group
(Devers)

NANCY

HAGUENAU

Rhine

STUTTGART

TUBINGEN

STRASBOURG

OFFENBURG

Fr First Army
(de Lattre de Tassigny)

MILES 0 — 40
KILOMETERS 0 — 60
FRONT LINE, 7 FEBRUARY, 1945
7 MARCH
10 MARCH
21 MARCH
28 MARCH
GERMAN POCKETS
ARMY GROUP BOUNDARY
ARMY BOUNDARY

THE ALLIED ADVANCE TO THE RHINE

M4 Sherman tank adapted to carry a flamethrower. This terrifying weapon was used principally against bunkers and reinforced defensive positions.

early in January 1945. On December 7, Eisenhower informed Bradley and Montgomery of his plan. Montgomery was to launch the main effort north of the Ruhr, while secondary efforts were to be made farther south by Bradley and Devers. What Eisenhower suggested was in effect a combination of both the "narrow front" and the "broad front" strategies, with the intention of reaching the Rhine River. Once the allies had secured bridgeheads across this barrier, they could drive into the heart of Germany.

Eisenhower's revised plan was possible because the Allied armies were now much better supplied Marseille and Antwerp had been reopened as major ports and the logistic infrastructure in France had been completed, which allowed supply depots near the front to be filled. Eisenhower could therefore think in terms of a general offensive right along the Allied line, with the exception of the steep and thickly wooded Ardennes sector, where Middleton's VIII Corps of the 1st Army was given a defensive role.

Hitler had other ideas and ordered a sweeping German offensive through the Ardennes with the object of taking Antwerp. If the German forces were successful, they could capture large amounts of supplies, especially fuel, and then destroy the three Allied armies northeast of the line from Bastogne to Antwerp via Brussels. General Ernst Brandenberger's German 7th Army would provide protection on the southern flank against any intervention by the 3rd Army, and the main German thrust would be made by General Hasso von Manteuffel's German 5th Panzer Army and SS General "Sepp" Dietrich's German 6th SS Panzer Army.

The "Battle of the Bulge"

The Germans waited until a spell of bad weather grounded Allied tactical air power. Then, they struck west on December 16 to start what is formally known as the Battle of the Ardennes, but is usually called the "Battle of the Bulge." The Germans committed 24 divisions, including

111

The 101st Airborne Division conducted an epic defense of Batogne during the Battle of the Bulge One paratrooper wrote letters home describing his unit's plight.

". . . two inches of snow on the ground and cold, still snowing. You are no more amazed than I! This is the first letter I've written since about the 18th. If I thought that on Xmas I'd be fighting the Krauts, think I would have gone over the hill! Ha Ha! Anyway, it looks as though we will. . . . miss your letters so terribly . . . no sleep, and no goodnight! . . .

Airmail Dec 22, 1944: Belgium 1430

". . . since my last note of the 18th it has been almost day and night straight through. Last night, however, I stretched out on the floor at 9.30 and didn't wake up till 0500. Shouldn't have slept that long, but no one woke me, I was about frozen, but fell good now, except still tired. The Jerries and us are at it again. The outfit is doing a good job in a difficult situation. No one has written since the 18th I'm positive. It couldn't be done, and couldn't be mailed. Lt. Bennett had a little tough luck. Should be back in a few weeks according to the doc. Julian is doing a very good job, as we expected. Talked to Bottomly, Homan, Pelham, Allworth, Sims, and Gregg today. They are fine. Hope they all continue to remain so. Stresser must have gotten lost, though I think he's O.K. Hope so. Nothing to get excited about . . . never did get but two Xmas packages. Hope the rest didn't get lost. The two were the box of assorted candy, and the box with the canned meats, cheese, etc. wrapped in red cellophane. It was so cute and pretty . . . telephones are right here in the Hdq and its' a busy place. The situation here is rather critical. We are not worried, particularly, because we gave the Krauts a very bloody nose

Tuesday and Tuesday night. Think it really hurt them. However, we are surrounded so it could be bad. No supplies or ammunition coming in. We have enough of each for about two days or to stave off one heavy attack. You should see Jerry tanks. God, but they are thick. Its' been quiet since noon, but what will happen tonight or this afternoon, don't know. Its' stopped snowing, but its' cold and the ground has quite a blanket of snow. Very pretty, but not convenient at all. Seems peculiar to be writing this when its' possible and almost probable that letter will never get mailed. Either get lost or destroyed, or something happen to me or to all of us. Except for poor clothing, and supplies, we are in good shape. Would have had those, but had to leave so quickly that we could not wait. This has been a peculiar campaign. My guess is that from here we'll go to Germany, pushing the Krauts till they quit. Looks like ground action now that we're here. Glad we didn't jump into this deal. . . . Bob Nelson, Lt. Col. whose artillery Bn. supports our outfit, just walked into tell us about the ammunition he doesn't have available. Well, hell, it could be worse, I suppose. Like Prunty used to say, "From the time you're born till you ride in the hearse, there's nothing so bad but it couldn't be worse". I'm not convinced! . . . have to stop now . . . will seal this and put it in my pocket and hope I can mail it someday . . ."

Airmail Dec 23, Belgium, 1500:

". . . just ran outside to watch the C-47's come in with our re-supply. This the first one to come in its' really beautiful! Never saw so many fighters up above. Its a clear, bright sunny day. The snow is coated on everything including my jeep which has no top or windshield. Only one plane was smoking. Guess it got it. We need the stuff. Have been cut off for two days now and have no rations, ammunition, or medical equipment. Help is close by though and the Aircorps is really working the Jerries over. Thunderbolts, Lightenings, and Typhics are going to town. We have hardly been hurt, though we've knocked out plenty of tanks and infantry. Julian and I ate the Xmas cheese and tongue you sent me. I threw them in my field bag, along with sardines you had sent. Now I have them when I really need them. And how good it tastes. They were still in the red cellophane and it was just like Xmas! . . . afraid we'll be pushing Xmas, though I hope we can get clothing before that. The men are almost frozen. Haven't heard anything from Stasser. Everyone else is OK except a few. The Krauts have had it, I think. This, I hope, is their dying kick. Then I can come home! . . ."

Airmail Dec 24th Belgium, 2100

". . . Tonight is so unlike on Xmas Eve that I keep forgetting about it completely. . . things have been rather rough. Whether or not they will get worse, I can't say. Probably not, though the future fighting might be worse later. Last night to give you a brief resume, was spent in sweating out a breakthrough by Jerry on our adjoining unit. That would expose our flank, so we had to move troops and get them dug in, etc. The ground is still frozen of course, and snow still on the ground. I got ½ hr's sleep last night. Hope we have no excitement tonight. Went to sleep some. Can just barely hold my eyes open now. The moon went down at 0400 and the Jerries pulled back, having gained nothing but inflicted losses on our men and equipment. They lost more heavily then we. About ten tanks were knocked out, including both sides, and it was quite

sticky. Today has been quiet except for some shelling and our Thunderbolts working all around us. An armoured column is trying to get through to us. It has our supply trains which we need badly. Things like blankets, overcoats (most of us have them) food, ammunition and medical equipment. We got a good resupply by the C-47s today. None were shot down. If we don't have to shoot a lot tonight we'll have enough by tomorrow night to stand quite a lot. Doc has plenty of medical equipment we found in the hospital here. This town, a few weeks ago, was way in the rear and had hospital units, and supply dumps. We just got here in time to pass through, meet the Krauts head on, stop, dig in, and hold. We got quite a lot of supplies which were here. The units up here before we arrived got chopped up badly, and stragglers keep coming in through our lines with awful tales of what happened. I hope our efforts, so far successful, in holding Bastogne, have been worthwhile. It must be a thorn in the High Command's side though they have by-passed us and gone on deeper and to the north according to the radio which is vague. We don't mind being cut off so long as we get re-supply by air and can hold the lines. If they crack our lines, it will end up a wild free-for-all which will be costly to both sides. Our tactics consider and expect encirclement, so it doesn't really worry us like a regular outfit. We don't like it, or course. Tonight, we have a meeting. It proved a lonely Christmas."

Following the Battle of the Bulge, the Americans resumed the attack on Germany. Sgt. Raymond Burgess recalls his lost fight with the 2nd Infantry Division in the winter of 1945:

The ground was frozen, so first you cleared the snow from the ground, try to break the dirt enough to plant a quarter pound charge of TNT, then blow the hole, and start digging. Everyone had a TNT package on his belt and fuses in his pocket. This was the way to start your fox hole. When we were preparing the ground someone had mentioned that the Germans usually had the cross roads zeroed in for their 88MM guns so you needed to be careful. The experienced men knew that because of enemy resistance in the area the digging of the fox hole was done as a defensive measure and to keep us busy.

About the time the first man was about to blow a hole in the ground, in came the 88's. We were safe for the time as the shells were landing up and down the road about one hundred yards away. With a pause in the shelling, everyone ran to the barn which had walls about a foot thick of brick and rock which would have given some protection. When we got in side, we found German prisoners waiting to be transported to the stockade.

One of the disadvantages was that very few Americans could speak German so communication with the Germans was not possible. Talking to German prisoners was out of the question, and it was not our job to do so. When the prisoners were taken back they would be questioned under military procedure for information which could help our cause. The prisoners were like us except for the uniforms. Wars are mainly based on political disagreements. The soldiers are fighting to win the war, but it is in self-defense, rather than being mad at or hating anyone. The feeling towards the prisoners was one of being in the same place at the time and they appeared more scared of the German shelling than we were.

After the shelling had stopped, we were ordered out and this time moved north of the main road. We walked in single file for a distance. Everyone turned east and started across the open field at about 1600 hours. We were crossing the field and up the hill to continue our push into Germany. The regiment's next objective was the town of Hellenthal. In the middle of the field was a barbed wire fence and someone said be careful as this is a good place for an ambush because you can become entangled in the wire and be an easy target. This did not happen, but another two hundred feet, as we started up a slight incline came the sound of heavy machine-gun fire.

It caught us by surprise. A hundred feet to my left a number of men were falling; some grabbing their heads and then were still. They walked directly into the gun implacement. Now everyone was hitting the dirt or in this case snow for protection. The gun was well concealed and everyone was firing toward the noise.

Then I was hit in the leg, more like a bee sting. The bullet must have just missed my buddy's head by inches. We traded rifles as he felt mine was in better condition than his. Later the rifle was placed in the ground to indicate an injured or dead person. Before the machine gun was knocked out there were seven Americans killed. Later I saw about twenty wounded Americans back at the barn which served as an aid station. "Buddies" referred to here was the group of men who lived, ate, and worked together. It was not anything special and except for this short time we were together (our lives depending on each other) I never saw any of them again.

As I lay there in the snow not knowing what to do, my buddy told me to "stay where you are I will mark the spot," and they will pick you up as soon as they can. The rest of the troops were pulled back to the road to my right. They had called for mortar fire to disable the machine gun implacement. I did hear the mortar shells go off. I do not recall thinking of anything except to wait for someone to come and help me. The next time I remember was hearing someone call, "is there anyone out here." I waved my arm, and they came over to say they thought I was dead. I was placed on a slide and moved over to the road, down the road to the barn. As I went I could see all the other men lined up on the road about to move out again. What I did not know was that at this time, the shooting war was over for me.

Later I had a chance to think back on that January day and knew that someone was watching over me that day. As I mentioned before that as we left our holding position and moved out, I lost track of time. Time had no meaning, no purpose. I have no idea how long I was out in the snow. I did not even think of trying to stop the flow of blood. The bullet had travelled in the right path, no broken bones, no arteries cut, and little loss of blood. It had passed through the upper thigh and just below my hip joint and came out on the inside of my leg. When the men picked me up in the field, they never bothered to give me first aid, but waited until I was back in the aid station. God had to be watching over me that day for which I am thankful.

ten Panzer divisions, in the 5th and 6th SS Panzer Armies, including a first wave of eight Panzer divisions against VIII Corps. The exhausted 28th and 106th Infantry Divisions took the full weight of the German onslaught and were shattered.

The American position looked worse than it was. As the Germans poured through the breach, the 4th Infantry Division held firm on the southern shoulder of the salient that the Germans were creating, while in the north, V Corps played a similar role after breaking off the offensive it had launched against the Roer River dams on December 13. Bradley rushed in two armored divisions as immediate reinforcement to check the momentum of the German advance, and Eisenhower committed the SHAEF reserve, made up of two airborne divisions which were recuperating at Reims after Operation "Market Garden."

The divisions arrived by truck on December 19. Ridgway's 82nd Airborne Division was thrown into the defense of the salient's northern side, and Brigadier General Anthony B. McAuliffe's 101st Airborne Division was sent to hold Bastogne against the advance of the German 5th Panzer Army. Montgomery

U.S. paratroops hit German positions with white phosphorus bombs from their 3·2-inch mortar in the French Alps in December 1944.

began moving a British corps to hold the line of the Meuse River, and at Bradley's order, Patton broke off his attack in the Saar and wheeled his 3rd Army north against the Germans' left flank.

Absolutely essential to the success of the German effort were the early captures of Saint Vith and Bastogne. At Saint Vith, Brigadier General R.W. Hasbrouck's 7th Armored Division checked but could not halt the German 6th SS Panzer Army, allowing V Corps to present an impenetrable front on the Germans' northern flank. VII Corps raced southwest in a successful effort to halt the German spearheads short of Dinant and the crossings of the Meuse River. Farther south, the Germans took the 18,000-man garrison of Bastogne under siege on December 26. The same day, the weather improved, and Allied tactical air power began to decimate the German forces, which were now running out of fuel and ammunition.

The 101st Airborne Division Holds Bastogne

The siege of Bastogne lasted until January 2, 1945, and decided the fate of the German offensive. Hitler refused to consider the suggestion of Model's Army Group "B" that the weight of the offensive should be shifted from the German 6th SS Panzer Army to the German 5th Panzer Army, which was making better progress, and so made eventual German defeat in the Ardennes inevitable. The initiative now passed to the Allies, and the six American corps holding the northern and southern sides of the salient began their counteroffensive on January 3. One of Patton's armored divisions had already broken through to relieve the defenders of Bastogne, and by January 16 the German salient had been destroyed.

It was the last offensive the Germans were able to mount against the Allies. This disastrous episode had cost the Germans about 120,000 men killed, wounded, and missing, as well as 600 tanks and assault guns, 6,000 other vehicles, and 1,600 aircraft destroyed. Allied losses, almost all of them American, were 7,000 killed, 33,400 wounded, 21,000 captured or missing, and about 730 tanks and tank destroyers ruined. While the Allies were able to make good their losses in men and materiel with little difficulty, the Germans could not. The German losses were com-

A panoramic view of the Dutch town of Nijmegen after bombardment by American and British artillery. In the background is the bridge over the Waal River, one of the 82nd Airborne Division's two main targets in Operation "Market Garden." The airborne soldiers could not take the bridge immediately; it took a combined assault by American and British forces on September 20 to gain this important objective.

pounded by the fact that they had scraped the bottom of the manpower barrel to bring their assault forces up to strength with high-quality troops, and these men were irreplaceable.

The Germans did take advantage of the American preoccupation with the Ardennes to strike the 7th Army's salient which was pointed at Karlsruhe in the Lower Vosges inside the angle of the Lauter and Rhine rivers. The 7th Army had been forced to extend its line north to cover the gap left by the movement of the 3rd Army against the Ardennes, and from January 1, it was pushed back to the line between Sarreguemines and Haguenau before checking the German 1st Army on January 17.

Advance to the Rhine River

Farther north, Eisenhower ordered the 12th and British 21st Army Groups to move up to the western bank of the Rhine River. As preliminaries, the British 21st Army Group cleared the Roermond area between January 15 and 26, while the 12th Army Group moved onto the upper reaches of the Roer River between January 17 and February 7.

This paved the way for Eisenhower's Rhineland campaign, which was designed to put the Allies on the western bank of the Rhine River between the North Sea and Switzerland. Eisenhower planned the campaign in three phases. The first phase involved the British 21st Army Group, with the Canadian 1st Army launching Operation "Veritable" southeast from the Nijmegen bridgehead to close a pincer movement at Wallach and Rheinberg. The 9th Army's Operation "Grenade" would move northwest from the Maastricht "appendix" of the Netherlands. When this major move was underway, the 1st Army was to take the Roer River dams and so shield the British 21st Army Group's southern flank. The second phase involved the 12th Army Group in the three-pronged Operation "Lumberjack": the 1st Army was to move from its position on the northern shoulder of the Ardennes in two diverging axes directed northeast at the Rhine River below Koln and southeast at the Rhine near Remagen.

The 3rd Army was to attack northeast from a point north of Trier parallel to the Mosel River toward its junction with the Rhine at Koblenz. The third phase involved the 6th Army Group, whose 7th Army was to drive northeast from Saarbrucken toward the junction of the Rhine and Main rivers at Mainz; at the same time, this group was to eliminate two German pockets on the western bank of the Rhine, south of the point at which the Lauter River flows into it opposite Karlsruhe.

Success All Along the Front

The first phase of the campaign began on February 8. As the Canadian 1st Army moved forward, it made only slow progress because of the sodden ground and appalling weather. The 9th Army's offensive was delayed when the Germans flooded the Roer River valley, but was then very successful when Simpson launched his forces on February 23. In just five days, the Americans broke through into open territory and linked up with the Canadians on March 3 at Gelder. By March 10, the last German positions west of the Rhine in the British 21st Army Group's sector had been destroyed.

The second phase was initiated on February 8, when the 1st Army started a drive that took it through the Hurtgen Forest, protecting the 9th Army's right flank and rolling up two German armies before it took Koln on March 6/7 and sent forces south to link up with the 3rd Army. Despite his instructions to conduct an "active defense," Patton behaved with his normal aggression, and drove the 3rd Army through the inhospitable Eifel region, captured the Westwall between the Lorsheim gap and the Mosel River, and pushed his leading element to the Rhine River opposite Neuwied on March 7.

The Bridge at Remagen

The most important single American episode of the Rhineland campaign was the capture on March 7 of a partially destroyed railroad bridge over the Rhine at Remagen. It was found and quickly

THE FINAL GERMAN RESISTANCE IN WESTERN EUROPE

Opposite: The final stages of the war against Germany saw the armies of the Western Allies moving east to link up with the Soviet forces advancing to the west.

Left: With a 0·3-inch Browning Automatic rifle at hand, an American soldier mans the 0·5-inch heavy machine gun on a half-track and waits to fire at any German aircraft trying to attack the all-important bridge over the Rhine River at Remagen after it had fallen into Allied hands on March 25, 1945.

captured by a two-battalion task force of the 1st Army's 9th Armored Division, and by nightfall the 1st Army had established a sizeable bridgehead on the eastern side of the Rhine River. The 1st Army enlarged the bridgehead as fast as it could against determined but uncoordinated German attacks, throwing new bridges across the river against the inevitable moment that the damaged German span finally collapsed.

As the 1st Army raced against time at Remagen, the 3rd Army cooperated with the 7th Army in a series of multipronged attacks with armored divisions in the van. Between March 11 and 21, these two armies cleared the Palatinate region of the last German forces west of the Rhine River. The final element to disappear was the German 1st Army's bridgehead between Mannheim and Karlsruhe. Evidence of the deteriorating quality of the German defense is provided by a simple statistic of the Rhineland campaign: for losses of less than 20,000 men, the Allies had taken the entire Rhineland, in the process killing and wounding 60,000 Germans and capturing 250,000 more.

Eisenhower had long ago decided to give the British 21st Army Group the main

part in the Allied invasion of the German heartland, because the North German Plain would be considerably easier to cross than the mountainous region south of the Ruhr. Eisenhower had to modify his plan when, as a bonus, the bridge at Remagen was captured, but he felt sure

With the town still under German artillery fire, American infantry in Remagen use the cover of buildings to move forward.

U.S. engineers haul an LCVP out of the Rhine River above Remagen. The craft had been used in the successful effort to stretch a net across the river to prevent German mines from drifting down onto the bridge.

Below: Bridging a major water course presents problems for the military engineer. The fast-flowing Rhine River was a particularly daunting challenge. This heavy pontoon bridge is able to carry tanks as well as trucks.

that the Allies' best opportunities lay in keeping the main weight of the offensive in the north. At this time, the Allies could deploy 85 strong divisions against just 60 German divisions with poor-quality manpower and minimal numbers of heavy weapons.

Patton Jumps the Gun

Patton had other ideas, and on March 22, the 3rd Army's commander threw his 5th Infantry Division across the Rhine at Oppenheim, using bridging equipment and naval landing craft brought up by his army logistical net. The operation cost only 34 men killed and wounded, and the 3rd Army engineers worked so effectively that, only two days later, four divisions were across the river. By March 28, the 3rd Army had created another crossing at Boppard, 40 miles downstream, with its spearheads at Lauterbach, about 100 miles east of the Rhine after bypassing Frankfurt-am-Main and wheeling northeast.

One day after Patton began his advance, Montgomery began to hurl his British 21st Army Group across the Rhine near Wesel. The British 2nd Army crossed at Wesel, preceded by the drop of two airborne divisions including Major General William Miley's 17th Airborne Division, and on March 24, the 9th Army crossed at Dinslaken. By March 26, the British 21st Army Group was crossing over 12 bridges, and two days later, it was streaming east around the northern side of the Ruhr after breaking the Germans' last-ditch defensive position at Haltern on the Lippe River.

Engineers of the Light Pontoon Company constructed this bridge beside the ruins of the Argonne River Bridge near Gerona on the drive to Manila.

A diver prepares for an underwater task during the repair of a bridge near Aachen which had been destroyed by the Allies in an effort to impede the German retreat.

On March 25, the 1st Army broke out of its Remagen bridgehead, and three days later, its armored forces had advanced 70 miles to reach Marburg on the headwaters of the Lahn River.

On March 26, the 6th Army Group became the last of the three army groups to plunge over the Rhine River. The 7th Army crossed in the area between Worms and Mannheim, and fanned out to the east on the 3rd Army's southern flank.

Eisenhower Switches His Emphasis to the South

Eisenhower saw the advantages of altering his long-standing strategic plan to exploit the advantages offered by the Rhine River successes of the 1st and 3rd Armies. On March 28, he ordered the 12th Army Group to push through central Germany, without thought to Berlin, in the direction of Leipzig and points to the southeast where the Soviet forces were already arriving. The Ruhr was to be encircled and destroyed by the 9th Army on the British 21st Army Group's right and the 1st Army on the 12th Army Group's left, leaving the British 2nd and Canadian 1st Armies to drive across the

North German Plain in the direction of Hamburg. The 6th Army Group was to advance down the valley of the Danube River with the task of eliminating all German resistance in an area thought by the Allies to be earmarked by the Nazis as a last redoubt, probably in the German-Austrian Alps.

The final campaign moved ahead smoothly as the Western Allies advanced east to meet the Soviets on the line of the Elbe River. The progress of the powerful armies was complex and far-ranging, but can be visualized accurately from the map on page 118. The first American troops to meet their Soviet counterparts were men of the 1st Army, who encountered Russian forces at Torgau on the Elbe River during April 25.

Germany Surrenders

During the last weeks of the war in Europe, the Germans suffered enormous casualties and surrendered in droves. Hitler refused to consider surrender, but he committed suicide on April 30 and was succeeded by Grand Admiral Karl Donitz. Donitz immediately started surrender negotiations, which were finalized on May

The conference between Churchill, Roosevelt, and Stalin at Yalta in the Crimea in February 1945 decided the basic political shape of post-war Europe.

Technician 5th Grade, 2nd Armored Division, 1944

U.S. armored units began to receive specialized clothing in 1941. The first issue was the waist-length tanker's windcheater jacket in waterproofed cotton with a blanket lining and knitted wool collar, cuffs, and waistband. The jacket was very popular with armored formations, and it was also coveted by the officers and men of other branches of the service. The initial version of the jacket had two large patch pockets on the sides, while the later version introduced vertical slash pockets. Though this man is not wearing them, in the winter of 1943-44, tankers were issued with heavy padded overalls that had a "bib" front, but these pale olive drab overalls were later revised and given a straight waist without the "bib." In 1941, the original russet leather helmet with a "doughnut" pad around it at brow level was replaced by the type illustrated. This tanker's helmet was painted green. Made of stiff leather, it was pierced for ventilation and had a high domed top to protect the wearer's head from knocks inside the tank. The earphone flaps were held in place by leather-covered flat springs and elastic straps snap-fastened to the rear flap. The overshoes came in several types. A civilian pattern of black ubber with metal snaps was popular, while another had rubber soles and heavy leather uppers, laced at the front. Rank chevrons and a and a divisional marking were worn on the upper sleeves, and personal equipment seldom included anything more than a pistol belt with a holstered 0·45-inch (11·43-mm) caliber M1911A1 automatic pistol, clip poches, and a first-aid kit.

7/8, and the war with Germany ended at midnight on May 8, 1945.

Tactical and Strategic Air Power

A major contribution made by the U.S. Army to the war in Europe was air power of two basic forms. Tactical air power made an enormous contribution to the success of the American ground forces, especially in Italy and northwestern Europe. Fighters such as the Lockheed P-38 Lightning, Republic P-47 Thunderbolt, and North American P-51 Mustang kept Axis fighters at bay, but were also capable of sprouting underwing loads of bombs and rockets in their other role as fighter bombers to provide the ground forces with very close air support. Heavier offensive firepower was delivered tactically by light and medium bombers, typified by machines such as the Douglas A-20 Havoc, Douglas A-26 Invader, North American B-25 Mitchell, and Martin B-26 Marauder. These aircraft carried a substantial bomb load, but also sported an increasingly heavy battery of fixed forward-firing guns to strafe Axis

ground forces. The tactical air forces that operated these and other planes grew steadily in strength and operating capability, and by the end of the war, each American army group was supported by its own tactical air force.

Given the importance attached to long-range heavy bombing in pre-war plans in the United States, it is not surprising that strategic bombing also featured very strongly in American plans and operations. From late 1939, the British had concluded that the superiority of fighters over bombers operating in daylight made it essential for bombers to operate by night. Accuracy, both in navigation and in attack, inevitably suffered, so the Royal Air Force's Bomber Command switched the emphasis of its attacks from pinpoint targets, such as specific shipyards, to area targets such as whole cities that included such shipyards.

The Role of the Heavy Bomber

The Americans were sure that their two main heavy bombers, the Boeing B-17 Flying Fortress and Consolidated B-24

The camouflage and markings help to identify this machine as a Consolidated PB4Y-1, the maritime patrol version of the B-24 Liberator. The plane was photographed over England on its way to an antisubmarine patrol in the Bay of Biscay.

The Boeing B-17 Flying Fortress, the most celebrated bomber used by the U.S. Army Air Forces in the European theater. Total production was 12,731 aircraft including 512 examples of the B-17E (the first truly mass-production model) and 3,405 examples of the B-17F (2,300 built by Boeing, 605 by Douglas, and 500 by Lockheed Vega). The type illustrated here is a B-17E, a development of the B-17D with a larger rear fuselage and revised tail surfaces of the distinctive pattern adopted by all later Flying Fortresses. The B-17F was an improved version of the B-17E with a number of modifications, including a frameless nose transparency. The B-17E spanned 103 feet 9 inches, was 73 feet 10 inches long and 19 feet high, and its empty and normal take-off weights were 32,250 and 53,000 pounds respectively. It was powered by four 1,200-horsepower Wright R-1820-65 air-cooled radial piston engines, and with them it reached a maximum speed of 317 miles an hour at an altitude of 25,000 feet, and a range of 2,000 miles with a 4,000-pound bomb load. The offensive armament contained 17,600 pounds of bombs, and the defensive armament included 12 0·5-inch machine guns in twin-gun tail, dorsal, and ventral turrets, single-gun waist and nose positions, and a 0·3-inch gun in the dorsal hatch. The crew was ten men.
Right: A bombadier in the nose of a Boeing B-17G.

Lieutenant General Carl A. Spaatz commanded the 8th Army Air Force in England. From January 1944, he was commanding general of the Strategic Air Forces, which included the 8th Army Air Force and the Italian-based 15th Army Air Force. From July 1945, he fulfilled the same task against Japan as commanding general of the Strategic Air Forces in the Pacific.

Liberator, using the advanced Norden bombsight, had the defensive firepower and high-altitude performance to fight their way through screens of Axis fighters and then deliver their bombs with pinpoint accuracy. This confidence convinced the Army Air Force that daylight attacks were a better solution to their plans, which were designed to reduce the war-making capability of the Axis powers by destroying key industries (ball-bearing factories, oil refineries, aircraft plants, etc.) and communications (railroad classification yards, bridges, tunnels, etc.).

The first U.S.A.A.F. formation slated for the European theater was the 8th Army Air Force, whose advance guard arrived in the United Kingdom during March 1942 under Major General Carl A. Spaatz, with Major General Ira C. Eaker's VIII Bomber Command and Brigadier General Frank O. Hunter's VIII Fighter Command as its major components. At first, the plan was to increase the force to 3,500 aircraft to act as support for the planned invasion of 1943. This ambitious plan was disrupted at an early stage when the Allies decided to invade French Northwest Africa, where the 12th AAF was later established.

The 8th AAF cut its operational teeth in a raid against the rail yards at Rouen on August 17, 1942. Thereafter, the unit began to mount a small but growing campaign against targets in northern France and the Low Countries, which was as far as the bombers could be escorted by early versions of the P-47 Thunderbolt. The American bombers soon built up useful experience and got promising results, but it became clear that the bombers' ability to defend themselves was not as good as American planners had forecast.

In October 1942, Major General Eaker was instructed to concentrate his VIII Bomber Command against the German U-boat pens in France. The campaign was waged until June 1943, but it was a waste of effort as the bombs of the period were not adequate to destroy the pens.

The "Pointblank Directive"

During this period, the Casablanca Conference produced a blueprint for a combined bomber offensive designed to hammer Germany and Italy by day and night. The "Pointblank Directive," issued after the conference, gave American and British bombers the primary objectives of U-boat construction yards, aircraft production facilities, transportation, oil plants, other war-making industries, U-boat bases in western France, northern Italian industries, and warships in harbors. The directive was reviewed at the Trident Conference of May 1943, and the definitive directive issued in June 1943 intensified the combined bomber offensive and added the desirability of destroying German aircraft in the air.

At about the same time, Thunderbolts which were able to carry a belly tank were introduced. The range of this important escort fighter's radius increased from 230

Women were quickly given previously "male" tasks such as aircraft maintenance during the war. Photographed at the Naval Air Station Whiting Field in Florida during 1944, these WAVES (Women Accepted for Voluntary Emergency Service) are servicing a North American SNJ trainer.

miles to 375 miles, which allowed the American bombers to fly slightly deeper into Europe. This added a useful number of targets in northwestern Germany to the 8th AAF's scope. From June 1943, the 8th AAF extended its effort into Germany. Its first raid was directed against Wilhelmshaven on June 11. In July, the 8th AAF extended its operations in Germany to aircraft production plants, which resulted in a major, though only temporary, reduction in deliveries of aircraft to the German air force.

The Ploesti Oilfields

By this time, Spaatz had been moved to command the Northwest African Air Force, and Eaker had assumed command of the 8th AAF. On August 1, he launched a major attack against the Romanian oilfields at Ploesti. The raid involved 177 B-24D Liberators that took off from Benghazi in North Africa for the longest strategic bombing raid yet attempted. The attack became disorganized in its last phases, but was pressed home with great courage. The raid did considerable damage, but it was mostly superficial and the complex was soon back to peak production. The unit lost 41 bomb-

ers over the target and another 13 as the planes approached or departed from the area, as well as a large number that were damaged, including seven that were forced to land in Turkey.

The Schweinfurt Raid

A comparable fate befell the 8th AAF raid of October 14 against the ball-bearing industry at Schweinfurt in Germany. This mission was flown by 288 bombers in two waves. The first wave achieved some surprise, but the Germans still attacked it strongly. Now thoroughly alerted, the Germans responded even more effectively against the second wave, and total losses were 62 bombers lost and another 138 damaged, many of them irreparably. The implications were clear for daylight strategic bombing beyond the range of current escort fighters, and deep-penetration raids were halted until the definitive escort fighter, the P-51 Mustang, appeared in December 1943.

From January 1944, the Allies took the air war to Germany with a vengeance. Lieutenant General Spaatz now led the U.S. Strategic Air Forces, which included the British-based 8th AAF and the

The North American P-51 Mustang, one of the greatest warplanes ever produced, was the escort fighter that made American strategic bombing in Europe a practical proposition. This 8th Army Air Force example photographed over England is a P-51B, the model that introduced the superb Merlin engine designed in the United Kingdom by Rolls-Royce and also produced in the United States as the Packard V-1650. This fighter carries a row of ten victory markings under the cockpit.

Arguably the finest all-round fighter plane of World War II, the North American P-51 Mustang resulted from a British specification. It first flew in October 1940 with a 1,100-horsepower Allison V-1710-F3R inline piston engine. The craft reached maturity with a Packard-built version of the Rolls-Royce Merlin engine. It became a classic interceptor, escort, reconnaissance, and attack fighter notable for its high outright performance, excellent handling, and very long range. The definitive model of World War II was the P-51D, the type illustrated here. It accounted for 7,966 of the total of 15,469 Mustangs built. Powered by one 1,510-horsepower Packard V-1650-7 Merlin liquid-cooled inline piston engine, it attained a maximum speed of 437 miles an hour at an altitude of 25,000 feet, and a range of 2,300 miles. The armament included six 0·5-inch machine guns in the wings, and 2,000 pounds of bombs or six 5-inch rockets under the wings.

Right: The firepower of the Mustang in its final form was six 0·5-inch heavy mavhine guns carried as a trio in each wing. The two inner guns each had 400 rounds, and the four outer weapons each had 270 rounds. The guns were harmonized so that their fire was concentrated on a single point ahead of the fighter, where their effect on other aircraft was devastating.

Italian-based 15th AAF. The combination of the American daylight raids and the British night sorties tore at Germany whenever the weather permitted, and they began to play a major part in blunting Germany's ability to wage a sustained war. Larger fleets of improved bombers with powerful escorts were important in this effort, but so were the greater skills of combat-experienced airmen operating under commanders who now had the skills to direct the right forces against the right targets.

The "Big Week"

Between February 20 and 26, the 8th AAF's "Big Week" was designed to strike at German industries, but also to tempt German fighters up into the air where they could be engaged and destroyed in large numbers. Five days of operations cost the Americans 244 bombers, but the Germans lost 692 fighters in the air and many more aircraft on the ground. German industry recovered quite quickly from the blow and soon delivered new aircraft to

Opposite Top: Taken in April 1946, this photograph reveals the extent of the destruction in the harbor of Marsielle before the Germans surrendered. The French and Americans cleared the damage so that the port could be used, but made no immediate effort to rebuild any of the facilities.

Opposite Bottom: Aircraft played a major part in defeating the menace of the U-boats in the Atlantic. Caught on the surface during July 1943, this boat is being raked by heavy machine gun fire as it attempts a crash dive.

Above Right: Lieutenant Vernon L. Richards of Felt Mills, New York, at the controls of his North American P-51D Mustang over England.

Below Right: The navy's counterpart to the Mustang was the Grumman F6F Hellcat. It saw comparatively little action in the war against Germany, but was a decisive weapon in the war against Japan.

replace these losses. What the Germans could not replace, however, were the skilled pilots who had flown many of the fighters that had been destroyed. The raids continued from March to May, when Germany lost 2,442 fighters in action and another 1,500 to other operational causes or on the ground.

In May, the heavy bombers were redeployed to tactical support of "Overlord" and returned to their primary role only in July. Between then and the end of the year, the American and British bombers topped the strategic bomber offensive with a truly decisive campaign. Their main targets were Germany's oil-production facilities and transportation system, though other important targets were steel plants, power stations, and weapon factories. There is now little doubt that the German armies, starved of fuel and supplies by the bombing campaign, were far less capable of halting the progress of the Allied armies. This effort continued into 1945, and by the beginning of April, there were so few worthwhile targets left that the strategic bombers turned once more to a tactical role in support of the ground forces, who were now only weeks away from crushing Germany.

With the war in Europe over, the United States could turn its full attention to the final destruction of Japan.

Glossary

Aircraft carrier: The type of warship that took over from the battleship as the world's most important military ship during World War II; in essence, it is a floating airfield. A substantial number of aircraft can be kept on board, maintained and operated by trained naval personnel.

Army group: Largest field formation, made up of two or more armies.

Battalion: A basic subdivision of a regiment, generally less than 1,000 men, commanded by a lieutenant colonel.

Battleship: The premier ship of World War II, with heavy armament and heavy protection.

Beach-head: The designated area on an enemy shore which is seized and held in an amphibious assault to allow additional troops, equipment, and supplies to be landed.

Blockade: A naval campaign to close the enemy's ports and coast, to cut off access or departure.

Brigade: A basic subdivision of the division, made up of two or more regiments commanded by a brigadier general.

Camouflage: The art of, and equipment for, concealing men, vehicles and weapons from observation from the ground or the air.

Combat command: A subdivision of the armored division, capable of semi-independent operations through its combination of armored, infantry, and artillery elements.

Corps: A primary component of the army, made up of two or more divisions. In the U.S. Army a corps is commanded by a major general, but in most other armies, the commander is a lieutenant general.

Cruiser: A long-range warship between the destroyer and the battleship in size. It has two basic forms: a light or unarmored cruiser for raiding merchant shipping with 6-inch guns and a heavy or armored type with guns of 8-inch or greater caliber for fleet operations.

Destroyer: A comparatively small warship developed from the torpedo boat. It has torpedoes and guns of about 5-inch caliber and is used for independent or fleet operations. The destroyer relies on speed and agility to avoid enemy fire, not on armor to withstand such fire.

Division: The smallest army formation, made up of two or more regiments and commanded by a major general. It is the basic organization used for independent operation and therefore contains support elements (artillery, engineers, etc.) in addition to its infantry.

Flank: The extreme right or left side of a body of troops in a military position.

Formation: Any large body of troops with a capability to operate independently from the rest of the army. It therefore possesses (in addition to its organic infantry units) a full range of artillery, engineer, and support services. The smallest formation is generally the division.

Howitzer: A piece of artillery designed to fire its projectile at an angle of more than 45° above the horizon, so that the projectile comes down on the enemy at a very steep angle.

In the van: In the leading wave of advancing troops.

Interdiction: Isolating or sealing off any area, principally to prevent the enemy from using the area as a line of approach to the battlefield.

Lodgement: Name given to a beachhead after it has been consolidated and expanded to incorporate airfield, port, and communication facilities. From a lodgement, sustained offensive operations can be launched against the enemy.

Logistics: The science of planning and carrying out the movement of forces and their supplies.

Materiel: The overall term for equipment, stores, supplies, and spares (from the French).

Munitions: The overall term for weapons and ammunition.

Rangers: U.S. Army personnel specially trained to carry out raids in enemy territory.

Regiment: A basic tactical unit subordinate to the division. It is made up of two or more battalions and generally commanded by a colonel.

Salient: An area that projects into enemy territory across the notional straight front line.

Strategy: The art of winning a campaign or war by major operations.

Tactics: The art of winning a battle by minor operations.

Unit: Any small body of troops which is not capable of operations independent of the rest of the The largest unit is the brigade (see also Formation).

Bibliography

Bailey, Ronald H. *The Air War in Europe.*)
(Time Life Books, Alexandria, VA, 1979).

Davis, Franklin M., Jr. *Across the Rhine.*
(Time Life Books, Alexandria, VA, 1980).
The last Anglo-American offensive in Europe.

Esposito, Vincent J. (ed.). *The West Point Atlas of American Wars 1900-1953.*
(Frederick A. Praeger, New York, 1959).
A fine map book coordinated with easy-to-understand text.

Goolrick, William K. and Ogden Tanner. *The Battle of the Bulge.*
(Time Life Books, Alexandria, VA, 1979).

Hine, Al. *D-Day, The Invasion of Europe.*
(American Heritage Publishing Co., New York, 1962).
For younger readers..

Hoyt, Edwin. *The GI's War.*
(McGraw-Hill, New York, 1988).
The real war, the European experiences of the common soldier.

Irving, David. *The Destruction of P.Q. 17.*
(Simon & Schuster, New York, 1968).
The destruction of a convoy on its way to Russia.

Keegan, John. *Six Armies in Normandy.*
(Viking Press, New York, 1982).
A master historian tells the story of D-Day to the liberation of Paris.

MacDonald, Charles B. *Company Commander.*
(Infantry Journal, Washington, 1947).
A young soldier's memories of small unit combat.

Marrin, Albert. *The Airman's War.*
(Atheneum, New York, 1982).
For younger readers.

Patton, George S. *War as I Knew It.*
(Houghton Mifflin Co., Boston, 1947).
America's foremost warrior's story.

Pitt, Barrie. *The Battle of the Atlantic.*
(Time Life Books, Alexandria, VA, 1977).
Convoy duty versus German submarines.

Pyle, Ernie. *Ernie's War, The Best of Ernie Pyle's World War II Dispatches.*
(Random House, New York, 1986).
The writings of the GI's favorite combat journalist.

Ryan, Cornelius. *A Bridge Too Far.*
(New York, 1974).
Popular history full of human interest anecdotes on the Arnhem operation.

Ryan, Cornelius. *The Longest Day: June 6, 1944.*
(New York, 1959).
Popular history of D-Day.

Sears, Stephen W. *Air War Against Germany.*
(American Heritage Publishing Co., New York, 1964).
For younger readers.

Terkel, Studs. *The Good War: An Oral History of World War Two.*
(Pantheon Books, New York, 1984).

Trevelyan, Raleigh. *Rome '44.*
(Viking Press, New York, 1981).
The battles of Anzio and Cassino and the drive to capture Rome.

Wallace, Robert. *The Italian Campaign.*
(Time Life Books, Alexandria, VA, 1978).

Weighley, Russell F. *Eisenhower's Lieutenants.*
(Indiana University Press, Bloomington, IN, 1981).
The campaign in France and Germany, 1944-45.
Good on organization and leadership.

Wright Michael (ed.). *The Readers Digest Illustrated History of World War II.*
(Readers Digest Association Ltd., London, 1989).

Index

Page numbers in *Italics* refer
to illustration